Listening children think:
exploring talk in the early years

Edited by Nigel Hall
and Julie Martello

Hodder & Stoughton
A MEMBER OF THE HODDER HEADLINE GROUP

British Library Cataloguing in Publication Data
A catalogue record for this title is available from the British Library

ISBN 0 340 65831 2

First published 1996

Impression number	10	9	8	7	6	5	4	3	2	1
Year		2000		1999		1998		1997		1996

Typeset by Multiplex Techniques Limited, Orpington, Kent.
Printed in Great Britain for Hodder & Stoughton Educational, a division of Hodder Headline Plc, 338 Euston Road, London NW1 3BH by Bath Press.

Contents

Contributors

Martin Coles is Senior Lecturer in Education at Nottingham University, UK.

Diane Fenton is Senior Lecturer in Education at Manchester Metropolitan University, UK.

Carol Fox is Principal Lecturer in Education at Brighton University, UK.

Sue Freeman is a primary school teacher in Sussex, UK.

Julia Gillen is a research student in the School of Education at Manchester Metropolitan University, UK.

Rob Greenhall is Principal Lecturer in Education at Manchester Metropolitan University, UK.

Nigel Hall is Reader in Literacy Education at Manchester Metropolitan University, UK.

Geane Hanson is an Assistant Professor at Hamline University, St. Paul, Minnesota.

Kate Holden-Sim is Research Assistant on the Punctuation Project at Manchester Metropolitan University, UK.

Pat Hoodless is Senior Lecturer in Education at Manchester Metropolitan University, UK.

Liz Jones is a Research Fellow in the School of Education at Manchester Metropolitan University, UK.

Charmian Kenner is an educational researcher at Southampton University, UK.

Julie Martello is Lecturer in Early Childhood Education at the Charles Stuart University in Sydney, Australia.

Kay Wells is a Language Support teacher in Lambeth, London.

Helen Williams is a nursery teacher in Lambeth, London.

Introduction

Young children chatter! Sometimes so much so that parents and teachers cannot resist telling them to shut up. Yet what are children supposed to do – their world is primarily an oral one. From birth to the age of around five or six their primary means of getting things done is to use talk or physical action. But talk is so complex that it takes years to truly master its complexities. How are children supposed to develop into competent talkers if they cannot practise their talk and, more importantly, how are they to learn to use language to think if they lack the opportunity to use it?

Talk is not learned as are many subjects in school through ritualistic repetition, through decontextualised exercises, or through endless drills. For the most part talk is learned not by being studied but by being used as a means to many ends. Children have to learn it that way: parents do not possess the linguistic knowledge that would enable them to instruct children in all the skills of oral language. As children use talk purposefully so they express their identity, they learn, they assert themselves, they establish relationships, they request and they use their talk to achieve many other human states.

This book is not about language development; there are many books already which examine the developmental progression involved as children learn to talk. This book is about children between the ages of three and seven using talk to get things done in their lives. Because younger children are using talk rather than writing, that talk offers a special access into their thinking. However, to make use of that opportunity, teachers and parents have to listen. They have to hear beyond the apparently seamless flow of sound and appreciate what is being revealed.

Although the chapters in the book are presented continuously, they nevertheless fall into a number of sections, although the sections overlap in many ways. In a section by itself is Martin Coles's opening chapter which sets out to overview the importance of talk in the lives of children as people and as learners. In the second section, three chapters have as their focus the examination of the ways in which children use talk in the process of acting upon the world. As young children talk in the bath, explore the world of the telephone and act as story tellers, so talk accompanies the exploration. In the third section, four chapters examine children using talk to reflect upon aspects of the world. The children in these chapters reveal their thinking about daydreaming, narrators in stories, how punctuation works and what time is. Too often children's own insights into complex concepts are seen as trivial, stupid, or simply wrong. These four chapters show that children are capable of exploring complicated concepts in subtle and profound ways. Finally, come two chapters which have the teachers as their focus. However, what these teachers are concerned about is the talk of their children and their own relationship to that talk. They show that listening to children demands more than just hearing the sounds they utter.

The factor that all these chapters have in common is the willingness of their authors to spend time listening to children talk and to learn about the children from their talk. The book is not about assessing children's talk but about understanding what happens when children talk. Young children's learning can never be understood properly if teachers will not spend time listening to the children. Finding time to listen in increasingly overloaded teacher lives is difficult; we do understand that. But not finding any time to listen to talk is to miss out on a vital opportunity to learn about children's thinking.

1

The magicfying glass: what we know of classroom talk in the early years

Martin Coles

Introduction

I remember very clearly the moment when it dawned upon me how important children's talk was to their learning. I was walking with my three-year-old daughter in the snow. She had never seen snow before. As she walked her wellingtons sunk in so deeply that the snow came over the tops. 'Dad, Dad,' she said, 'the snow is jumping up at me.'

Ever since then I've kept a notebook of stories, incidents and information about children's talk. It includes the small girl who called me over to her table where she was looking through a huge, Sherlock Holmes-type magnifying glass. 'Come here, come here,' she said, 'come and look through this magicfying glass.' It also includes a child who told me that a hexagon was a circle with corners and a five-year-old boy who, in the middle of a school lunch, apropos of nothing, stumped me with the question, 'Where were you when the sun was built?' All these are examples of children trying to come to terms with their world. They are working out through language, and the responses to it, how their world is.

It is right, I think, to have an eye and an ear for the fun of working with small children. And it is right to keep hold of humour and use it to interpret and alleviate the difficult times that occur in all classrooms. But, just to adopt the attitude, 'Gee don't children say the darndest things,' is simply to position yourself as an audience for children's talk, and of course, teachers have a responsibility to do more than that. A teacher's responsibility is to try to understand a child's language and, in particular for teachers of young children, to understand how we demand a different kind of language in school from that used in the home. There is often a large discrepancy between school talk and talk in the world outside of school. It seems to me very important that we take this into account in our teaching if we are to help young children in their language development and in their use of language for learning.

Talk in the classroom

Since any curriculum is conveyed by classroom talk and since any curriculum presents to children a picture of the world with implicit priorities which push some elements of experience and action into prominence and obscure others (Barnes, 1989, p.45), the importance of talk in the classroom cannot be exaggerated. This importance has been reinforced by the rediscovery of Vygotsky's work (1961 and 1978) which alerts us to the cognitive benefits that interactive talk gives young children.

On the other hand, discourse analysts have revealed that much classroom talk is in fact constraining and deeply conservative. A substantial body of work describing classroom talk, much of it done in the 1970s, makes it obvious how much of talk is concerned with keeping control and managing social relations rather than with pupil learning. This research suggests that teachers tend to take little account of the dynamic nature of context and its personal and actively constructed character, little account of the context presented by the co-presence of other learners, and even less account of the everyday knowledge pupils bring with them to the classroom. All this is reflected in the communicative style of their teaching.

Let me repeat to you a story told to me by Prof. Charles Desforges to make the point clearer.

1 *The magicfying glass: talk in the early years*

A boy from a strict home enters school in the reception class and loves it. The teacher has lots of attractive things to do, and most important of all he gets to choose (something he is not allowed to do at home). At the end of the first day the teacher asks, 'Would you like to clear up now?' and the boy, remembering he has a choice, decides that he would rather not. He carries on with his activity. The teacher, of course, sees incipient disobedience. She walks up close to him and whispers fiercely in his ear, 'I said clear up. Now do it!' How does the boy make sense of that experience?

Concern about classroom talk goes back more than twenty years when Barnes (1969) found a predominance of factual questions and very few which demanded reasoning as a response. He suggested this indicated that teachers are more concerned with regurgitating material which has been handed over ready-made than with encouraging pupils to participate actively and think for themselves. Barnes and Todd (1981) found that when pupils were left to discuss problems without the teacher present, the quality of their thinking and understanding improved. Where the discussion failed, it was sometimes because the competitive atmosphere in the classroom intruded. Keddie (1971) concluded that it is the failure of high-ability pupils to question what they are taught that contributes in large measure to their formal achievement.

More recently Tizard and Hughes (1984) have shown how young children's natural enthusiasm for learning cooperatively is suppressed in favour of the teaching priorities of the school system. They suggest that during the first year in school, children spend as much as fifty per cent of their time on solitary tasks prescribed by the teacher and that by the third year, sixty-six percent of time is spent this way, and the rest of the time is spent for the most part, passively attending to teacher talk. Bennett and Dunne (1989) found in the course of their research that:

> What generally passed for group work was in fact collections of
> children sitting closely together, but engaged in individual tasks.
> In such groups the level of cooperation, frequency of
> explanation, and knowledge exchange is low. (p.8)

The observations of McManus (1987) in reception classes over a one-year period confirms the work of Tizard and Hughes and suggests that much of what Barnes and others found in secondary schools is present in almost fully developed form from the start of schooling: talk is dominated by a teacher's need for control:

'Right, it's table-toys time.'

'Right, now it's news time.'

'It's nearly milk and biscuits time.'

He describes one incident:

> The children had to play appropriately. To a boy pushing a plastic block along the floor with his foot: 'Harry, they're not for kicking, they're for building.' To a girl who is lifting and dropping a box lid: 'We don't want that, Jaspreet. We don't come here for that.' During news time the children had to conform to the teacher's structure in order to present their news. They were called out in front as the rest were shushed – a minor ordeal that wiped some of their minds blank. (p.25)

It seems that the level and degree of teachers' control of language in the classroom means that there is little room left for pupils to determine for themselves what constitutes valid talk.

The central issue

As children are learning to use talk, they are also learning about their role as speakers (Halliday, 1978). Adults know more than children by virtue of having lived longer, so it is inevitable that in adult/child conversations the child is more often than not going to be cast in the role of receiver rather than giver. This is not necessarily a bad thing; there are many situations in the real world where a degree of asymmetry in talk is entirely appropriate, for example, it is reasonable that a doctor asks more questions of a patient than a patient does of the doctor (though there would be concern about the balance of the relationship if one were to find a situation where the patient did not get a chance to ask any questions).

Clearly, children need to be informed by adults in many instances. A problem arises though when this particular form of asymmetry, what Phillips (1985) calls the asymmetry of knowledge, occurs without any balancing experience, and in combination with discourse asymmetry, as for instance when adults always decide what a child means.

1 *The magicfying glass: talk in the early years*

Wells and Nicholls (1985) describe a conversation between Mark, a pre-school child, and his mother. When he says 'jubs bread' ('jubs' being a word he often uses for birds), his mother replies 'Oh look...they're eating the berries, aren't they?' In this instance, if Mark did in fact mean 'bread' then he has learned that his mother will sometimes decide his meanings for him. The point is not that it is wrong for an adult to step in when a child is struggling to make meaning, nor does what I am arguing here contradict the findings of Tizard and Hughes (1984) who suggested that children are very often partners in dialogue with their parents, but even children who have sensitive carers and teachers will have learned that adults are potentially authority figures with the ultimate right to sanction meanings. In a classroom, where adults place fairly heavy constraints upon children's linguistic freedom, perceptions are bound to harden. As Phillips points out, early messages about the asymmetry of their own conversational rights will take root when children hear teachers using linguistic strategies such as asking closed questions (Hammersley, 1977 and Alexander, 1992), insisting on specialised linguistic registers (Barnes, 1976), and making evaluative follow-up moves to every answer a child gives (Sinclair and Coultard, 1975).

Importantly, there is evidence that children can already engage in reasoned thinking prior to school through peer-group conversation. Before the age of six children can formulate simple hypotheses, for example, 'If we had a real one and your Daddy had a real one it would be good.' (McTear, 1981, p.127) Children as young as three will ask for clarification of meaning (Garvey, 1975). Four-year-olds will offer alternative suggestions if they do not agree with what their peers have said (Shields, 1980). It is important, of course, that we know young children are able, in conversation with their peers, to question, make suggestions of a hypothetical nature, challenge, and so on, but it is equally important to realise that they perceive peer-group discourse as an opportunity to use language in these ways; and, that it is normal to do so. Since the discourse status of the members of the group is equal, they learn to collaborate in order to make meaning, using language in the range of ways just described. It is not that they could not use language in these ways with adults, it is simply that they are less likely to do so since adults are perceived to be more knowledgeable and thus less open to challenges, questions, suggestions etc. Unfortunately, this perception of the asymmetry inherent in adult/child talk is reinforced in their normal experience of the classroom.

The long traditions of hierarchy, competition and individualisation in schools make establishing new social contexts for learning a difficult task. Releasing the power of dialogue between children is one way of breaking the barriers of those traditions. This implies establishing experiences which promote opportunities for children to talk, reason, and argue with each other, and which promote less passive forms of learning. When children engage in dialogue with each other, they are compelled to reflect, to concentrate, to consider alternatives, to listen closely, to give careful attention to definitions and meanings, to recognise previously unthought of opinions, and in general to engage in a vast number of cognitive activities that they might not have engaged in had the discussion not taken place.

What are the most memorable and stimulating moments of the school day? Assemblies? Pencil and paper tests? Or, discussions in which children are involved and talking about what matters to them? Following such talk they reflect on what they themselves have said; they recall what others have said and try to figure out why they might have said it; they reproduce in their own thought processes the structure and progress of discussion. This is what is meant when it is said that thinking is the internalisation of dialogue.

When we internalise dialogue, we reproduce not only the thoughts that we have just heard the other participants express, but we also respond in our own minds to those expressions. Further, we pick up from the dialogue the ways in which people draw inferences, identify assumptions, challenge one another for reasons, and engage in a range of intellectual interactions with one another.

Of course, this description is an ideal. Not all instances of talk between children work like this. Children are perfectly capable of giggling, chattering, not paying attention, or starting to talk all at once. Even when they all talk in sequence they may listen to what each has to say and try to build upon one another's contribution; but these problems are matters for creative consideration, not rejection of the whole notion. The other chapters in this book demonstrate that it is possible to organise classrooms and curriculum activities in a way which recognises the importance of talk between pupils.

I want to make it clear that I know most teachers are aware that children need the opportunity to talk. Most teachers do not want to treat children as if they were mindless tape-recorders, but even though this issue of learning through talk has been on the educational agenda for more than twenty years, and despite the fact that there will be few teachers who would deny the importance of talk in helping pupils of all ages to learn and demonstrate their learning, it does not happen very often. In the words of Alan Howe, director of a national project on the topic, 'There is a shadow which falls between the idea of the value of collaborative talk and the reality of classroom practice.' (1988, p.7)

It does us little credit if we ignore or deny firm evidence; rather, perhaps we should consider this evidence as a first step to improving the situation. So I want briefly to explore four internationally known studies of young children's talk in order to fill in the picture I have been drawing; they are research studies which provide clues to how the problem explained above can be solved.

The four research studies

Study 1

Barbara Tizard and Martin Hughes (1984) contrasted young girls' language at home with their mothers, with their language experience in the nursery. They found that whereas children at home had extensive conversations with adults in which they built up shared meanings and tested out ideas, such conversations rarely occurred at school or at nursery. This was partly because there wasn't time, and partly because the teacher and child didn't have the initial shared experience that make such conversations possible.

The following passage from their book *Young Children Learning: talking and thinking at home and school* is not, I'm afraid, happy reading:

When we came to analyse the conversations between these same children and their nursery teachers, we could not avoid being disappointed. The children were certainly happy at school, for much of the time absorbed in play. However, their conversations with their teachers made a sharp contrast to those with their mothers. The richness, depth and variety which characterised the home conversations was sadly missing. So too was the sense of intellectual struggle and of real attempts being made on both sides. The questioning, puzzling child which we were so taken with at home was gone. In her place was a child who, when talking to staff, seemed subdued, and whose conversations with adults were mainly restricted to answering questions rather than asking them, or taking part in minimum exchanges about the whereabouts of other children and play materials. (p.9)

The overall conclusions of the study were these:

- that teachers inhibited much decision-making and negotiating behaviour;

- that teachers asked questions rather than engaging the children in conversations;

- that talk was mainly about tasks/play work rather than the rich variety of situations that were discussed at home;

- that teachers were more intent on pursuing their own educational agendas than offering children the chance to explore the world at their own level.

The schools in which they did their studies were far from being poor ones. It is just that children's school language lives were devoid of a qualitatively high level of oral interaction and the intellectual effort which they put into sorting out the world at home.

Study 2

The second British study was carried out by Gordon Wells (1985). He was interested in how children's pre-school language contributed to their learning and to their later school achievement. He collected a very large amount of taped talk from 128 children. Wells's conclusions are in agreement with those of other researchers. He found that, compared with homes, schools were not providing an environment that fostered language development. For no child in Wells's study was the language experience of the classroom richer than that of home – not even for those believed to be linguistically deprived. One example from Wells's work (p.158) will illustrate his findings. He presents the following as a typical example of a classroom conversation:

Lee	I want to show you. Isn't it big! (Lee brings a chestnut.)
Teacher	It is big isn't it? What is it?
Lee	A conker.
Teacher	Yes.
Lee	Then that'll need opening up.
Teacher	It needs opening up. What does it need opening up for?
Lee	'Cos the seeds inside.
Teacher	Yes, very good. What will the seed grow into?
Lee	A conker.
Teacher	No. It won't grow into a conker. It'll grow into a tree won't it? Can you remember the ...
Lee	Horse chestnut.
Teacher	Horse chestnut. Good. Put your conker on the nature table then

Wells comments:

> Our objection to this, and to countless other similar conversations... is not that teachers are concerned to extend their pupil's knowledge, but that they are so concerned to do so that they never really discover what it is about the experience that the child finds sufficiently significant to want to share in the first place. Children's experience of how adults engage in conversation with them in the years before they come to school has not been like this. The result is that many of them are bewildered by the new situation where they suddenly find themselves expected to fit in with someone else's definition of what is interesting and to learn what someone else prescribes. It is not surprising therefore, that some children become tongue-tied and appear much less competent than they really are.

What these two pieces of research suggest is that what is most important in the behaviour of adults who are with young children is:

- sensitivity to the child's current state, and an understanding of the child's level of ability and immediate interests;

- sensitivity to the meanings he or she is trying to communicate; and a desire to help and encourage interaction where both participants have equal space and discourse status;

- the ability to be a sympathetic listener rather than a propensity to dominate the situation and make it adult led;

- skill in responding to the meaning intended – just as a good conversationalist would with people of any age – and to have genuine concern to achieve a mutual understanding.

In other words, children learn best from adults when the adult sees their own role as being to assist the child's performance, which is what happens in homes.

Study 3

The third study was also carried out some years ago, but the findings remain highly relevant. Susan Phillips studied the classroom talk of Native American children in a school on the Warm Springs Reservation in Oregon (1972). Teaching these children was difficult since they hardly talked in class and the situation did not change as they got older.

Phillips's careful observations suggested to her that this problem was a result of the disjunction between their experience of talk and learning outside school and what was required of them in the classroom. In the community from which they came the learning traditions were to do with silent watching and listening and practising skills privately, so children felt threatened when teachers asked them direct questions which they had to answer in front of the rest of the class. In the community, social activities were organised informally by anyone who was interested, rather than by people with particular positions. There was not, for instance, any distinction between audience and performers in the community singing and dancing. So children were very uncomfortable in a situation where the teacher was perceived to control their talk and where they were asked to perform. In school, the children of Warm Springs were faced with language practices which were very much at odds with the beliefs they had acquired at home about how people should relate to each other. The teachers in the schools, understanding this, gradually moved their practice more towards the experiences that children were used to outside school, avoiding whole class discussion, and such activities as show and tell, and including more small group work where individuals could try out things in a less intimidating atmosphere.

Study 4

The fourth project is the classic inquiry carried out by Shirley Brice-Heath and described in her book *Ways With Words* (1983). Heath studied the language experience of pre-school children in three small but contrasting American communities. In relation to our concerns in this chapter it is the findings relating to children from Trackton, a black working-class community, which have the most relevance. At home, these children were used to much oral storytelling; they were comfortable interacting with an audience, and they were exposed to a great deal of adult discussion to do with texts, such as newspaper articles and church-related items. In their community people asked questions about whole events with answers usually involving the telling of a story or the making of comparisons with other events. In school, however, children were asked questions about details and individual features (colour, shape, size) and, rather like the boy from the strict home in the story earlier, were asked questions which were really commands – Why don't you stop talking now and start writing? So again, there was a gap between the talk of the home and that required at school. The school did not in fact value the children's language.

Teachers often lost patience with the type of response that children had been used to giving at home, telling a story and linking two situations metaphorically. However, the consequence of the rejection by the school of children's language use resulted in them losing confidence and eventually switching off school altogether.

Obviously schools are not homes. Schools have different physical and social characteristics. Most significantly there are higher adult/child ratios in school than in the home. And there are language experiences that are not related to homes which schools quite properly provide. Indeed Tizard and Hughes (1984) have argued that it is not necessarily a bad thing that there is a gap between home and school language. In saying this they are taking into consideration the argument Margaret Donaldson makes in her famous book *Children's Minds* (1978), where she argues that children must eventually learn to communicate with others who do not share the same home experiences; that schools have a duty to introduce children to new knowledge and ways of thinking, and in particular that schools should be helping children to learn how to understand the world in a decontextualised way.

But none of this is to say that it cannot be anything but helpful for teachers to know about and understand the home language practices of their pupils and, especially in the early years, to find ways of organising their classrooms and the talk within them to bridge the gap between children's home experiences and the language practices they will need to acquire in order to cope with school. There are strategies which can be adopted with talk to individuals, with groups and in whole-class discussions that would improve children's learning.

The first is to do with responsiveness, careful listening, and an attempt to try to understand a child's meaning and then to extend and develop it. In other words, to collaborate in talk with children, to act as facilitator rather than dominating the language interaction.

The second is to avoid, as far as possible, imposing an adult point of view. The 'teacher knows best' response pre-empts children's attempts to make meaning and undermines their confidence to work things out themselves. Being prepared to wait for a child's response longer than is usual in classrooms would be a significant step in the right direction, even if the silent space feels uncomfortable at first.

The third is to develop the skill of asking questions that foster reflectiveness on the part of the child (not those which simply ask the child to guess what is in the teacher's head). Questions should aim to help a child develop and explore his or her thinking rather than act as a test; they should be asked as a way of facilitating the child's communication.

The problem with so much classroom talk is that it is the teachers and not the children who ask the questions, and in practice many of the questions, and question formats, teachers use inhibit intellectual activity. When questions always originate with the teacher (or with a publisher) and when the resolutions and answers are always ones sanctioned by the teacher, there is little incentive or opportunity for pupils to develop an intellectual spirit. The 'passages of intellectual search' which Tizard and Hughes (1984) recognised in the home conversations where children were often allowed to take the lead in asking questions, rarely occur in classrooms. Almost everywhere children are schooled to become expert at answering questions and are kept novices at asking them. And yet, given the opportunity, children are very good at asking significant, interesting and genuine questions (Rosenshine and Chapman, 1992; Van der Meij, 1993).

Talk and learning

There is a theory of language which understands it as a medium through which thought is conveyed. Meaning is out there. Some questions are founded on this view, especially those questions which are most common in school. They are the questions asked in order to have what the questioner knows reflected back by the questioned; questions which are used to maintain the status quo. Typical classroom discourse consists of this type of questioning. It is a discourse controlled by teacher questions which often demands quick, terse, factual answers and leaves little time for children to respond, elaborate or reason out loud. Perhaps this explains, in part at least, why some children do not learn how to express their ideas and formulate their thoughts. If the teacher asks all the questions, then he or she, and not the pupil dictates the course of events: what will be thought about and when. But as language and thinking are fused in verbal reasoning, so some children, lacking expertise in the process of creating coherent, disembedded or decontextualised accounts of what they know and understand, may appear intellectually incompetent while in reality they are still grappling with the problem of making sense to other people.

There is another view of language – that it is thinking; that meaning comes into being through language. In this view questions have a particular potency since their role is to help realise thought which is as yet unthought, which is only potential. From this viewpoint, (Halliday, 1978) children not only advance their linguistic abilities but in 'learning how to mean' also discover how to plan, evaluate and monitor their own intellectual activities. If this is true, then the nature and quality of classroom discourse plays a potentially vital role in developing a child's ability to learn and to reason analytically and to engage in purposeful, social language.

Major changes then are necessary if schools and teachers are to provide effective environments for talk. Teachers will have to radically overhaul their conception of their teaching role, and will need specific curricular time to develop productive talking environments because despite the primacy and universality of spoken language and its consequent claim to be the true basic in the curriculum, it is still the case that in terms of consistency in time allocation and attention, it is usually treated less well than reading and writing. This anomaly suggests that primary or elementary schools have in some sense a limited conception of educational priorities, despite all the rhetoric about child-centredness. Alexander (1984) explains the reasons thus:

> ...nineteenth-century mass compulsory elementary education [is] the institutional and legal (if not always ideological) foundation of modern primary education. That system of education aimed for basic levels of literacy and numeracy. The ability to use spoken language – to communicate, argue, reason, generate ideas, express and choose opinions and deepen understanding – was not only superfluous to the economic, occupational and political requirements of those who devised the system, but was potentially subversive of them. (p.62)

The need to cultivate independent and reflective thought in classrooms has always been central to progressive pedagogy, but teachers' classroom behaviour has not, so far, changed to accommodate this principle. A core of progressive teaching (project activities, small group work, merging two or more subject areas, more contact with the world outside school, more freedom to move around the classroom, varied classroom groupings) may have become standard practice in early years teaching, but the dominant pattern of instruction is still teacher-centred and the dominant mode of classroom organisation and management is still teacher talk. The fundamental authoritarianism of the elementary tradition, and the press towards coverage of subject matter persists in various forms. The life conditions of classrooms may have gradually changed, but that change has altered little else. The fundamental conditions for the encouragement of productive talk in the classroom are still too rarely seen. Perhaps though, the examples of talk described in the rest of this book are evidence that we ought to be optimistic about the possibility of change for the better and that we do not need to be afraid of children's talk.

In his book *Talking With Children* (1983) Ronald Reed takes a position with regard to children's talk which contrasts two familiar extreme positions. The first is characterised by the old saying 'children must be seen and not heard', suggesting that children are not fully-fledged people and that until they grow up they ought to play a spectator role, as if learning is something which happens primarily through observation. A contrasting view is characterised by the 'children say the darndest things' type of reaction I mentioned before. In this case children's talk is appreciated by adults, but ironically adults become the spectators who regard children's talk as a kind of entertainment. Reed's position is one that is now commonplace: that not to recognise the power of talk is to minimise the children's opportunities for learning by denying them the use of one of their most potent tools:

> People need to talk. Take talking away from them and you deprive them of something valuable. Take talking away from them when they are children and the process of education grinds to a halt. We must make space – a large space – in the curriculum where the need of a child to talk is recognised and encouraged. (p.120)

References

Alexander, R. (1984) *Primary Teaching*. Eastbourne: Holt, Rinehart and Winston.

Alexander, R. (1992) *Policy and Practice in Primary Education*. London: Routledge.

Barnes, D. Language in the Secondary School Classroom in Barnes, D., Britton, J. and Rosen, H. (1969, 4th ed. 1989) *Language, the Learner, and the School*. Harmondsworth: Penguin.

Barnes, D. (1976) *From Communication to Curriculum*. Harmondsworth: Penguin.

Barnes, D. and Todd, F. (1981) Talk In Small Learning Groups in Adelman C. *Uttering, Muttering*. London: Grant MacIntyre.

Bennett, N. and Dunne, E. (1989) Implementing Co-operative Group work in classrooms. Paper given at EARLI conference, Madrid.

Brice Heath, S. (1983) *Ways With Words*. Cambridge: Cambridge University Press.

Donaldson, M. (1978) *Children's Minds*. London: Fontana.

Garvey, H. (1975) Requests and responses in children's speech, *Journal of Child Language*, 6 pp. 423–42.

Halliday, M.A.K. (1978) *Language as Social Semiotic*. London: Edward Arnold.

Hammersley, M. (1977) School Learning: the cultural resources used by pupils to answer a teacher's questions in Woods, P. and Hammersley, M. (eds) *School Experience*. London: Croom Helm.

Howe, A. (1988) Small Group Work: the successful permeation of new ideas, *Oracy Matters,* 11. Wiltshire CC.

Keddie N. (1971) Classroom knowledge, in Young, M.F.D. (ed.) *Knowledge and Control*. London: Collier–Macmillan.

McManus, M. (1987) I said hands up, *The Times Educational Supplement*, 10 April, p.20.

McTear, J. (1981) Towards a model for the linguistic analysis of conversation, Belfast Working Papers in *Language and Linguistics*, 5, pp. 79–92. Belfast: Ulster Polytechnic.

Phillips, S. (1972) Participative structures and communicative competence in Cazden, C., Hymes, D. and John, V. (eds) *Functions of Language in the Classroom*. New York: Teachers College Press.

Phillips, T. (1985) Beyond Lip-Service: discourse development after the age of nine in Wells, G. and Nicholls, J. (eds) *Language and Learning: an Interactional Perspective*. Lewes: Falmer.

Reed, R. (1983) *Talking with Children*. Denver: Arden Press.

Rosenshine, J. and Chapman, J. (1992) Teaching Students to Generate Questions: a review of research on the effectiveness of different concept prompts. Paper presented to AERA: San Francisco (mimeo).

Shields, L. (1980) The implications for psychology of the study of dialogue skills in pre-school children. Paper given to the Warsaw Academy of Science, London University Institute of Education, Department of Child Education (mimeo).

Sinclair, J. and Coulthard, R. M. (1975) *Towards an Analysis of Discourse: the English used by Teachers and Pupils*. London: Oxford University Press.

Tizard, B. and Hughes, M. (1984) *Young Children Learning: Talking and Thinking at Home and School*. London: Fontana.

Van der Meij, H. (1993) What's the title? A case study of questioning in reading, *Journal of Research in Reading*, 16, 1, pp. 46–57.

Vygotsky, L. (1961) *Thought and Language*. Cambridge, Mass: M.I.T. Press.

Vygotsky, L. (1978) *Mind in Society: the Development of Higher Psychological Processes*, Cole, M.; John-Steiner, V. and Souberman, E. (trans. and eds). Cambridge MA: Harvard University Press.

Wells, G. and Nicholls, J. (1985) (eds) *Language and Learning: an Interactional Perspective*. Lewes: Falmer.

Wells, G. (1985) *Language, Learning and Education*. Windsor: NFER-Nelson.

2

Bathtime talk

Diane Fenton and Julie Martello

Background

The relationship between adults and young children varies across days, across weeks and across months. Sometimes adults have to control or chastise children; sometimes they are busy getting on with tasks and the relationship becomes a more formal one. At other times the world suddenly seems a more relaxed place and adults and children seem to talk to each other in ways that transcend other kinds of boundaries. Some moments are just more relaxed and adults and children talk to each other more as people. Teachers will recognise some of these moments; they often happen when children first arrive into the classroom before the day formally begins, when a teacher is on playground duty, or when a single child is helping a teacher during a play time. It is as if the more formal relationship between teacher and child is transformed as the setting itself departs from the formal teaching structure.

In homes as well, there are moments when, perhaps partly because of the setting, the talk between parents and children has the potential to move into a different register. Bathtime is such an event in the lives of many young children. Although young children's bathtimes can have their tense moments, they are more usually associated with warmth, fun, games and relaxation. They also usually tend to take place in the early evening and perhaps invite some looking back across the day. Bathtime, despite being a parental prescription which might not always accord with a child's sense of values, is usually both a very physical experience and a very language-dominated one. The following case study of bathtime was undertaken because we were interested in exploring how the talk might reveal some of the salient features of the relationships and the setting in this fairly typical, routine occurrence. To set the scene and explain some of the methodology for our case study, Diane describes the initial stage of the research.

Diane

In thinking unreflectively about bathtimes in our house it always appeared to be a setting where talk was encouraged and was always interesting. I have always enjoyed bathtime with my children, and when the opportunity arose to record some children's talk, bathtime seemed the perfect setting. I wanted a situation where I had the twins together, which was fairly self-contained and where talk was a major component. Bathtime seemed just the event and would, in addition, offer me the chance to explore some of my impressions about the talk which took place at bathtimes in my household.

Bathtime is always seen as a major part of the evening in our household. We do not have many routines but we do try to make sure the children have a bath each night. Apart from the reason of hygiene, it is the one time of the day when we can have the children's undivided attention and give them ours. There is no distraction from the television and we regard it as a form of 'quality time'.

We have three children: Natalie aged six, and twin boys, Matthew and Alex who have just turned three. The twins are fraternal and although they do look alike it is quite easy to tell them apart. They also have quite different personalities. Alex responds more to adults and older children whereas Matthew enjoys being with children of his own age. Alex prefers physical play while Matthew plays more with toys and especially enjoys role-play using his cuddly toys for characters. Alex loves to watch television and would sit for hours in front of the box if allowed, whereas Matthew gets bored with it quite quickly and wanders off to do something else.

The boys normally share a bath and whilst one of us is in the bathroom with them, the other can give Natalie some individual attention. Natalie has a bath on her own later, again allowing her more personal time with a parent. I decided not to use Natalie in our study, partly because I felt that she would know about and react to the presence of the tape-recorder, and partly because it would have moved the simplicity of the focus away from the twins.

The proceedings are fairly constant. The boys usually get changed in their bedroom as the bathroom is quite small. This can take anything from a few seconds to an hour depending on the kind of mood they are in. On average they spend about fifteen minutes in the water. Normally they go back into the bedroom to get dried and this can also take quite a while as they like to play with their toys at the same time and have a habit of treating the bedroom furniture as an assault course.

I decided to record only the bathing part of the proceedings as it is easy to see where this begins and ends, and as these sessions tended to last around fifteen minutes, it was a manageable amount of talk to transcribe and analyse. I decided to record every bathtime for a seven-day period.

There were some shifts in the context during the week of recordings. On the Tuesday I was delayed getting home and my husband decided to switch the recorder on and tape himself and the boys at bathtime. This proved to be a positive action adding a different dimension to the situation. Also, we decided to go and stay with my parents during the weekend so two of the sessions were taped in grandmother's bathroom which presented new distractions, namely a pumice stone, hand shower, bath brush and plastic duck! While the shift in circumstances during the week meant some variation in the way bathtime occurred, that is how it happens in life, so it seemed reasonable to take the recordings as they happened – warts and all!

The recordings were made on a small portable tape-recorder which was placed out of reach on a shelf. It recorded clearly and the machine was not noticed by the children, whose behaviour was unaffected by it in anyway at all. I am not sure that was true for me. I had the time to transcribe each of the first three sessions after the events. This was perhaps not such a good idea. I felt, after listening to the first evening's recording, that I had over-reacted to the presence of the tape-recorder and had adopted a very teacherish stance. I then tried to change my approach for the second bathtime. However, after listening to the energetic and fun time the boys had participating in water fights during their father's session, I again changed my style. From then I decided to take more of a backseat in the proceedings and decided not to listen to the tapes again until the week was over.

At the end of the week I had recorded almost two hours of talk. While that may not sound like much, it does in fact add up to a very complex collection of talk, and the problem with real talk is that it does not fall neatly into ready categories. It was at this point that the collaboration began in earnest. Julie explains in brief how the talk was analysed.

Julie

Because we wanted to examine the twins' talk in the context of their relationships and physical surroundings we needed a method of analysis which encompassed all of these factors. A functional approach was chosen because it does just this. It focuses attention on the functions of language, that is, the ways in which we use language to get things done in our daily lives. In considering how language is used to achieve a variety of goals, we have to understand the language system, English in this case, upon which we must draw in order to do this. As well, we need to acknowledge elements in the social context, such as the interpersonal relationships and the topic, which influence our choices from the language system. A functional view allows us to take all of these factors into consideration and to explore the interrelationships between the various factors. In contrast, simply identifying and quantifying the children's grammar or vocabulary development, for instance, does not acknowledge the purposes for which talk is used, the interactional nature of the talk and its location within a particular physical and social context.

Having chosen a functional approach, each of the seven day's transcripts was closely examined for what the children and adults were doing with language and how they were achieving particular purposes through language. On a first run through the

21

transcripts, a long list of functional categories was identified. These initial categories included ones such as: collaborating in play; asserting identity; asking for or giving information; and playing with words. Useful sources for this categorisation were the early works of Halliday (1977) and Tough (1976) who both described a range of personal and social functions for which young children use language. The adults' language was also categorised according to what they were doing with it, for example, whether they were redirecting the children's behaviour or getting on with the task of bathing. It must be stated here that any piece of language can have, and often does have, more than one function so an attempt was made to allocate utterances to the most appropriate category while acknowledging other possible functions. After categorising the talk in this way, comparisons could be made across the seven days and a search for patterns begun.

The nature of the talk

The transcripts contained instances of many language functions but it was clear that the children were using talk for some purposes far more often than for others. The same could be said of their parents' talk, given the obvious constraints of managing three-year-olds in a bathroom. After considering the language functions of both the children and the adults, five prominent aspects of the bathtime talk were identified, focusing on how the children used it: to negotiate the relationship between themselves; to express their plentiful needs and wants; to play physical and verbal games; to reflect on experience; and to subvert the intentions of the adults. As already noted, talk is rarely, if ever, achieving a single purpose, so a range of interrelated language functions is covered in each of the following discussions.

Cooperation and conflict

Being a twin can mean having a very close relationship with your other twin, but it can also, at times, mean being very competitive. While most parents want to treat their children as unique people with distinct identities, the problem with twins is that so much is done together that these boundaries are sometimes tested. It may be more of a problem for a parent of identical twins but it was still the case that these fraternal twins did most things together, even if only for family convenience. From the perspective of each of the twins, maintaining identity and being treated fairly is very important and any situation which forces both of them into a confined space for a set amount of time will probably test the ways they maintain identity and the ways they work together.

Not surprisingly for children of this age, we found that the twins interacted as much with their parents as with each other and often engaged in individual rather than cooperative play. Even so, there was a substantial amount of talk where the children invited, included, supported and cooperated with each other in play. As in the following example, most of these exchanges are short and show the children tacitly accepting each other's intentions as they play:

> Matthew   Don't put mine upside-down. (*Referring to boat.*)
> Alex   No I not.

and a little later ...

> Matthew   That's the green one. This is green. (*Pointing to a boat.*)
> Alex   This one's not going to sink. It's hit my knee.
> Matthew   These ones, these ones are racing.
> Alex   Oh. The yellow ones race.

While the overall tenor of the children's talk in relation to each other is one of friendship, there are also occasions where conflict arises out of differing preferences or deliberate transgressions. The conflict may be enacted physically but the language shows us how the children cope with these situations and even sometimes negotiate a settlement. In the example below Matthew attempts to stop Alex's infringements by first telling him to stop, then explaining how Alex's behaviour is affecting him, kindly assuming that Alex may not know this. Adult intervention is needed here, as it must often be with three-year-olds.

> Alex   Let me have it (teddy). Squeeze the water out.
> Matthew   Don't squeeze it on me will you, Alex.

and shortly afterwards ...

Alex	Fireworks! Fireworks! (Squeezing water out of teddy.)
Matthew	You doing it on me. You doing it on me, Alex.
Dad	Right, come on. You got me then. No, don't do that, Matt.

We can take heart, and some delight, in the seeming universality of scenes like this but we wonder how common it is to hear a three-year-old negotiating a successful solution to a conflict, as we found in the next extract:

Alex	Can I have it (*brush*) now, Matthew?
Matthew	No. I've got it.
Alex	Can I have it now, Matthew?
Matthew	Not yet.
Alex	Why?
Matthew	Have the duck. That's your duck.
Alex	Don't want it.
Matthew	Put it on there. It'll fall off. It needs a wash on that bit.

(He hands Alex the brush which has a spot to wash off.)

The strategy of offering an alternative plaything and the ability to share may have been learnt from parents or reflect individual personality but we think that this kind of talk to negotiate relationships among quite young children is a topic worthy of further research.

The bathtime talk also revealed other aspects of the twins' relationship with each other and with their parents. The notion of identity, mentioned earlier, includes both the desire for equal treatment and for acknowledgement of one's individuality. Talk which revealed both these drives was plentiful in the transcripts and was most obvious in the twins' sometimes conflicting desires to be the same and yet to be different. Whatever one has or wants, the other very often wants the same, particularly if it involves the attention of a parent. Although not always the case, in the following game context it was easy for dad to oblige:

(Dad has made soapsud beards and is 'shaving off' Alex's.)

Dad	Shall we shave? Zzzzz
Matthew	Shall we shave mine?
Dad	S z z z z
Matthew	Shave mine! Will you shave mine?
Dad	Shave yours? Let's have a look.
	Z z z z z z z. Will you try?
Alex	Will you do it to mine, Daddy?

Many briefer examples show a similar wish, often expressed by echoing the other's words, to have or do the same as the other twin:

Alex	Oh. My boat's upside down. It's not going. It keeps going upside down.
Matthew	My boat keeps going upside-down.
Alex	I've put my finger in the chimney (*of toy boat*).
Matthew	Let me do it. Put my finger in the chimney.

However, there are many instances when the twins disagree over what they want or like and seem to be demonstrating that they are separate identities. Sometimes, this is very obvious as when Matthew declares 'I'm Matthew', thinking that his father has mistaken him. At other times the need to act and be seen as a distinct person is realised in more subtle ways. Disagreeing with the other over colour preferences or declaring ownership and control of something may be ways of asserting that you are special and different. These are just three examples chosen from among many in the transcript:

Mum	Should I get you some towels ready?
Alex	Yes. I want a blue one.
Mum	I've got the blue ones ready.
Matthew	I want a pink one.

Alex	Can I have my boat in?
Mum	There's another one here.
Alex	No. That's not mine. I don't like yellow.

Alex	No! No! No! My, my boat (*crying out*)
	My boat. My boat. (*When Matthew takes his boat.*)

The examples show the children protecting their own interest by asserting ownership and control of objects and by insisting that others recognise their ownership, likes and dislikes. When conflicts do arise, it seems they are often caused by transgressions, or perceived transgressions, against this sense of self. Protection of the physical self is also a concern noted in the transcripts and complaints about being squirted come from both children and adults! Physical hurt, or complaint of it, occurs rarely here but one extract demonstrates how an accusation by Alex is of such concern to Matthew that he later attempts to clear the record. A few minutes earlier Alex had told his mother that Matthew had sprayed water on him and 'got it in my eye'. In the following game, Matthew refers back to the incident much to the puzzlement of Alex, who seems not to understand:

Matthew	A flying teddy! A flying teddy!
Alex	A flying teddy! (*Giggles from both.*)
Matthew	I didn't hurt you.
Alex	What?
Matthew	I didn't hurt you.
Alex	You didn't hurt me?
Matthew	No. (*Giggles from both.*)

This seems a poignant example which shows the value that Matthew places on maintaining a friendly relationship with his brother and the joy they both have in playing together. Conflict is bound to be a part of the twins' relationship but they are already developing some effective strategies for dealing with it. Matthew shows that he can use talk to refer back to an experience and reflect on it with his brother in order to clear up a misunderstanding. Successful or not, it's a strategy many adults might benefit from using.

Talk and the satisfaction of wants and needs

The need for friendly relationships is only one of the needs which the children's talk highlighted in the bathtime transcripts. As most three-year-olds do, the twins demonstrated a rather large list of wants and needs. The context obviously plays an important part in determining the kinds of needs and wants that the children express, so most were connected to the bathtime games and tasks.

Some physical needs, like toileting and drinking, were noted but the majority were requests for toys and help with the games which were a focus of all the recorded bathtime sessions. The games are discussed more fully in the next section. Here we were interested to note that there was not only a large list of objects and activities 'wanted', some repeated numerous times, but there was also a wide range of language used to express these desires. In fact, the language the twins use for this purpose covers all four possibilities in the English mood system: statements, commands, questions and negatives. Some examples from among the many recorded show how the children, at only three years of age, have already learnt to use subtle differences in their talk to achieve the purposes that are important to them.

Statements

> I want a beard.
> I want the yellow one *(Water wheel).*
> I need a wee.
> I want to go downstairs.
> Dry me.

Commands

> Let me get out! *(Of bath.)*
> Do it to me again, again Daddy. *(Shave beard.)*
> Put it out! Get it out! *(Duck.)*

Questions

> Will you put the boats in?
> Can you fit this in here, Mummy?
> Will you tickle us, Daddy?

Negatives

> Don't want the boats out.
> I don't want to play splashes.
> I don't want the soap to melt.

The children's expression of wants and needs are clearly related to their growing sense of identity and there are instances among the examples which demonstrate both their desire to be the same and have the same treatment as the other, and their desire to be different. They make statements and requests about their needs and are able to direct the actions of others, through commands, to help them achieve their aims. Being able to clearly state what they don't want is a well-developed skill which these children share with most other children of this age.

Talk for games and for the joy of it

By far the most common context for talk in the bathtime transcripts was that of games. In fact, for the children, bathtime seemed to signal playing and games and they often returned to the same games, triggered by particular toys or objects. For their parents too, bathtime was a time for fun and games as well as for the more practical and adult-oriented concerns discussed in the next sections. Consequently, the transcripts contain many examples of games where the children play with each other and with their parents. These games are often physical, involving toys, water, soapsuds, and are often accompanied by talk or word play. We were particularly struck by the amount, regularity and centrality of verbal play in the twins' games.

The physical games played by the children were usually accompanied by talk which could be called a running commentary; that is, it describes what the child is doing while he is doing it. Often, this was begun by one of the twins who was then joined by the other until the play became so wild that a parent's intervention was warranted. The following is a good example of this:

Alex	A flying car (*Throws car*).
Mum	I've not seen a flying car before, have you?
Matthew	A flying teddy. (*Throws teddy*). A flying teddy.
Alex	With a flying boat.
Mum	Careful! Someone's going to get hurt again if you're throwing, aren't you? Just see if you can make them go in the water, not in the air.
Matthew	A flying boat. A flying boat with a teddy in!
Alex	A flying car!

Matthew	A flying teddy!
Mum	That's a bit like *Chitty Chitty Bang Bang*, isn't it?

There are many occasions in the transcripts when the children use the repetition of single words to describe what is happening or to simply accompany an action. Sometimes, the word is related to what is happening, as with 'Sink. Sink. Sink.' (sinking boats) and at other times perhaps metaphorically related or not related at all, as in 'Bonfires. Bonfires. Bonfires.' (while squirting water) or 'A tangerine. A tangerine. A tangerine.' It seems that these words are repeated over and over for the sheer pleasure of it as they are often followed by giggles, especially when Mum expresses bafflement at their use.

Extended segments of word play seem to occur more often with parents and involve play with both meaning and repetitive sound. Once again, we found several examples of this kind of word/meaning play, sustained by parental questioning or participation, as in the following extract:

Alex	This is a nice teddy.
Mum	What's it called?
Matthew	This is called Bambi.
Alex	Mine's called Thomas the Tank Engine.
Mum	Your teddy is called Thomas the Tank Engine. That's a funny name for a teddy.
Matthew	Is it? Is it a train then?
Alex	No, it's a bee. (*Giggles.*)
Matthew	Is it a Thomas the Tank train? It's a Thomas the Tank train teddy.

Other examples of word/meaning play with parents show the children repeating a phrase over and over in a game context. When Mum is washing their legs the children begin to point to different parts of their body saying, 'Let's do that leg' (pointing to chest) and 'Let's do this leg' (pointing to neck). When their father has playfully threatened to squirt the boys using the words 'I'm warning you!' they take great pleasure in provoking him while repeatedly asking 'Are you warning me Dad?' The central role of games and, in particular, word games was a striking feature of the bathtime talk of both the twins and their parents.

Talk to reflect on experience and learn about the world

Another function of the talk we noted was its use to reflect on experience and learn about the world. This kind of talk was sometimes initiated by the twins and sometimes by their parents. The twins asked questions and used exploratory language to try to work out how things operated in the world. Of particular interest is the way talk was used to try to explain a phenomenon:

Alex	It (*boat*) keeps going upside down 'cos it keeps, fills, cos it fills, it's filling up with water.
Alex	It's all heavy.
Matthew	My horse is gone heavy. It's got a lot of water on.
Alex	It's got a lot of water in it. A lot of water in it.
Matthew	I'll squeeze mine out. It's not squeezed out.

This language is very tentative and we can almost feel the children grappling to understand as they try to put their meaning into words. By explaining to each other they are also explaining to themselves and clarifying their own understanding.

Asking questions was another way the twins used language to learn. When they were in grandmother's bathroom, many more questions than usual were asked about the new objects around them: pumice stone, brush, soap, bubble bath and shower hose and, as always, parents obliged with explanations:

Alex	What is it? (*Picking up pumice.*)
Dad	It's a pumice. It's to rub hard skin off you.

Just as a parent was always present to answer the children's questions they were also very visible throughout the transcripts as the initiators of exchanges. As both writers are teachers and parents of young children, we immediately noticed the large amount of parent talk, particularly the frequent use of questions of a 'teacherly' type. There was a distinct tendency to direct the children's talk towards particular topics and forms, for example, recalling the events of the day or providing information and explanation. In short, the talk the adult promoted was often of a kind valued in schooling. In some cases, a parent's attempts were successful but very often they were resisted by the children as our last section documents. When the adults did manage to engage the children in a sustained conversation they were able to support the children's language, through scaffolding questions and rephrasings. This creates longer exchanges and opportunities for the children to reflect on their experience of the world in a way that they are, as yet, unable to do alone. One example of this can be seen in the extract below:

Mum	What have you been doing? What were you doing with Daddy at the park to get dirty hands?
Alex	I just get an ice-cream, Mummy.
Mum	You had an ice-cream and your ice-cream made them that dirty?
Alex	No.
Mum	Well, what made your hands dirty?
Alex	I haven't had, I haven't had a dirty cone.
Mum	You didn't have a dirty cone. No.
Alex	No.
Mum	So what made your hands dirty at the park then?
Alex	I had some mud. I had some mud on.
Mum	You got mud on them, did you?
Alex	Yeh.

It took some time but eventually, with Diane's scaffolding, Alex is enabled to focus on the specific cause of his dirty hands and to recall his experience at the park more fully. In recalling the details for his mother, he is also revisiting them for himself and is more likely to remember and learn from them. This is one of the functions of the adults' talk in the bathtime context and, seen from an adult perspective, it is a worthwhile contribution. But perhaps the children's perceptions of their parents' conversational gambits might be different.

Talk and the subversion of adult intentions

The most amusing aspect of our analysis of the bathtime talk has been the emerging picture of the children holding steadfastly to their own line of play and resisting, often with a subversive humour, the efforts of their parents to direct their conversation or behaviour. In each of the seven transcripts there are occasions when the parent's questions are greeted with an uncomprehending 'What?', answered with a brief 'I don't know', washed over by the ongoing play or answered knowingly with an inappropriate response. We get a sense of the children being absorbed in their play and not wanting to be distracted:

Mum	What did you do this morning when Mummy was at work?
Alex	Nothing.
Mum	Did you not help Daddy outside in the garden? He was chopping trees down, wasn't he?
Alex	Yeh.
Matthew	It don't go in there (*Referring to a teddy*).
Mum	It goes in that one. We went to the park this afternoon, didn't we, when Mummy came home?
Alex	It's sinking! (*Returning to game.*)
Matthew	Mine's sinking in the water.

It has been mentioned earlier that the bathtime context places constraints on the adults' role as the children are very young and need to be kept safe and bathed. So there is a task to be achieved and often the adult talk is related to this task. However, it's the 'teacherly' questioning that the children seem to resist and subvert and we will end with a few interesting examples which suggest that the children know when they are being quizzed like this and that they delight in refusing to play along.

(Lots of splashing going on, nonsense talk and ignoring Mum.)

Mum	Did you eat all your lunch at nursery?
Alex	Yeh. And, and, and I eat it with this stick here. (*Giggles.*)

(Again lots of splashing, giggling and screaming.)

Alex	The water go out that way. (*Giggles and screams.*)
Mum	I think I'll use this white soap. (*Giggles and screams.*) Which animals did you like the best today? The sheep?
Alex	No. Giraffes.
Mum	We didn't see any giraffes!

Mum	What are you doing, Alex?
Alex	Doing the wall.
Matthew	Washing the wall down.
Mum	Well, did Nana ask you to wash the wall?
Alex	Yes.
Mum	Did she? Are you sure? Don't do it anymore.

Conclusions

This chapter does not tell us whether bathtime talk is significantly different from all the other situations in which talk is embedded. Nevertheless, it has shown that it offers a site where particular kinds of talk are used in powerful ways. The five aspects of bathtime talk discussed here may be common to many other similar households or unique to the case study. A more widespread study might reveal whether there are common features of bathtime and bathtime talk in a given cultural context. It might also show some interesting variations in bathtime talk both within and across cultural or social groupings.

This case study reveals that, for some children, bathtime is an opportunity to use talk for a range of purposes and to engage with a range of topics. It has thrown some light on the role of adults and the purposes for which they use talk in this situation. It also has a lesson for us in that even very young children can tell when adults are getting too prescriptive in their demands. Matthew and Alex have a long way to go in their careers as language users but their bathtime talk already reflects a wealth of competence as well as a willingness to experiment and play with language.

References

Halliday, M.A.K. (1975) *Learning how to mean – explorations in the development of meaning.* London: Edward Arnold.
Tough, J. (1976) *Listening to children talking: guide to the appraisal of children's use of language.* London: Ward Lock Educational.

3

'Don't cry, I ring the cop shop': young children's pretend telephone behaviours

Nigel Hall, Julia Gillen and Rob Greenhall

Background

The telephone is one of the commonest everyday objects. According to the British Telecom Press Office, around 90,000,000 phone calls are made each day in the UK using British Telecom lines (although this figure probably includes other kinds of communication using telephone lines such as fax). Around eighty-seven per cent of homes in the UK have telephone lines and these lines, in many cases, will have more than one phone on them. What percentage of the total calls are made in homes is not known but it is clearly going to be many, many millions each day. The telephone is a very visible object and is, of course, a very audible object. A telephone is not something which is hidden in a home. As a consequence, from an early age, children are attracted to it. The very act of making or receiving a telephone call seems intrinsically interesting to young children. Unlike many other objects in the home the telephone possesses great power; adults always respond to its summons.

From an early age, children are witnesses to telephone usage. This behaviour has certain characteristics which make it very accessible to young children. The telephone is usually located in a fixed position, it makes a noise, it is accompanied by certain unvarying responses or actions, and it involves talk which is directed towards the physical object of the telephone handset. In addition, the rair has very pronounced ritualistic qualities which render it susceptible to imitation.

The interest young children have in the telephone is indicated by the popularity of it as a toy. According to a recent full-page newspaper advertisement from British Telecom, one of the best selling lines of the toy manufacturer, Fisher-Price, is a toy telephone which rings and can be dialled. The toy telephone seems to be one of the standard props to be found in children's bedrooms and toy boxes. It is also one of the standard props of the early years' classroom. It is not always a toy telephone. Despite their adult size and weight, children seem to enjoy the added realism they bring to play settings. It is rare these days to find a nursery or kindergarten class without either a toy phone, a real phone doing duty as a play phone, or sometimes real phones linked to other phones within the school.

The questions

But what do children actually do with the phones? Despite their commonness and the many years that they have, in one form or another, been in school, there seems a total lack of evidence about how children use them. In recent years there have been many thousands of pieces of research about the development of children's language and about young children's play. Yet, when we come to look for research about young children's telephone skills it seems an unresearched topic.

The number of research papers on young children's use of the telephone can be counted on the fingers of one hand (Bjelic, 1987; Bordeaux and Willbrand, 1987; Holmes, 1981; Mininni, 1985; and Warren and Tate, 1992) and despite the frequency with which children use telephones for pretend purposes, we have been able to find on that topic only one brief extract from a longer paper (Garvey and Berndt, 1975) and some comments in Mininni (1985). It seems that it is such taken-for-granted behaviour that no one has found it worthy of, or interesting enough to, study.

So why are the telephones there in schools? Do they have an educational significance beyond being just another prop for socio-dramatic play? Have they any more status than the small pots and pans in the home corner? When we spoke to teachers there was general agreement that the children used them quite frequently, usually in socio-dramatic play, and seemed to enjoy using them. However the teachers were much less certain about whether anything was being learned or whether development of any kind was taking place. The teachers could see how telephones had some potential for encouraging talk but were not sure what learning was being demonstrated when the children used them.

In this chapter we hope to explore some of these issues. As part of a more substantial project investigating how young children learn to become telephone conversationalists we bugged a telephone in a play area and simultaneously filmed the area using a miniature video camera.

The recording was done in the socio-dramatic play area of a nursery class. Forty children were involved, twenty in the morning and another twenty in the afternoon. The children were aged three-and-a-half to four-and-a-half. The area was the Three Bears' Cottage and was divided into two. Half the area was the bedroom and the phone (for technical reasons) was placed in this half. A wall separated the bedroom area from the other half of the play area and thus, the video camera (and for the most part, the microphone) could pick up only what happened in the bedroom area.

The children's use of the phone

Non-linguistic behaviour

The correct use of the telephone needs certain non-linguistic actions. Children need to perceive the object as something which has communicative potential, lift the handset, hold the handset in the correct relationship to the mouth, know how to dial (and thus how to recognise and know numbers), know that one needs to speak and listen, and replace the handset after use. The three- and four-year-olds in this nursery all seem to recognise the telephone as an object for a specific communicative behaviour. None of them seemed to use the telephone in any other way. They did not build with it, throw it around, or behave in ways which treated it as a different kind of object.

During the week in which the play area was filmed a large number of calls were made. It might seem a simple matter to say how many but for various reasons it is quite difficult. Some calls are easy to identify: one child approaches the phone, makes a call and then goes away. In other situations two or more children were involved and, to complicate matters further, the phone was sometimes passed around. We judged there to be 128 episodes that could constitute a phone event, although some of these involved more than one child.

Of the forty children, eleven made no calls at all during the period in which we collected data in the play area. It is possible that the absence of telephone behaviour has more to do with the play situation than their willingness to use telephones as most of these children did use the telephone in another situation we examined. Only two of the children did not have a telephone at home, and both these children did make calls in the play area.

Of the pretend calls, only twenty-three (18.11 per cent) did not involve any dialling actions, although in those that did, the dialling occurred at different times; sometimes before a call and sometimes during a call. In only a relatively small number of the calls did the child actually say any numbers, although the absence of speech does not mean that the children were not thinking numbers as they dialled. Occasionally there was a specific reference to dialling and numbers as when one child said to another, 'No, you've rung the wrong number – phone number. I know the phone number.' Another instance was when one child terminated a phone event by saying, 'They're not there', and another child responded, 'That's because the wrong ... you've rung the wrong number.' All the children held the handset so that they spoke into, or listened to one of the ends of the handset. The average length of each event was 29.8 seconds but this ranged from calls as long as 137 seconds down to only two seconds (which involved little more than a child picking up the phone and putting it down again). In general it seems that these three- and four-year-olds knew about the physical behaviours associated with making a phone call, even though they did not always use them at the appropriate moment.

Knowledge of basic telephone language structures

The majority of the phone events involved talk. Only a very small percentage (8.6 per cent) of the phone events involved no talk. Some of the talk was very brief and sometimes consisted of no more than 'Hello – Goodbye' whispered or shouted into the handset. Other talk was much more sustained and more complex. The complexity was increased when telephone events involved two or more children in swapping the telephone around, and when they involved interaction with adults and children outside of the event.

Many of the children made simple calls which revealed a basic grasp of some essential language routines involved in making real telephone calls. Pam's call is a typical example (in this transcript words in square brackets represent speech which was unclear).

> *(Pam lifts up receiver.)*
> Hello, who's that?
> *(Pause.)*
> Minnie?
> *(Pause.)*
> Yes, hello.
> *(Pause.)*
> Yes.
> *(Pause.)*
> Why [don't] we go out?
> *(Pause.)*
> OK. Yes.
> *(Pause.)*
> I [won't/will phone] tomorrow, Bye bye.
> *(Replaces handset.)*

At first, Pam's behaviour seems so straightforward, obvious and simple that it is hardly worth commenting on. However, it does in fact deserve some closer scrutiny. Pam, aged three years and ten months, already seems to understand what has been termed 'the essential features of telephone discourse'. In this brief piece of telephone behaviour Pam has demonstrated knowledge of some of these typical telephone conversational features. She has an opening:

Hello, who's that?
(*Pausa.*)
Minnie?
(*Pause.*)
Yes, hello.

Adult telephone conversations usually have specific opening routines. The telephone ringing acts as a summons for the call to be answered. The receiver usually answers by an act of identification, 'Hello, 367 6983', and the caller then responds by revealing who is calling. Although in Pam's call there is no ringing, Pam goes through something of this ritual. Although she does not identify herself, she requests an identification from the caller using a questioning intonation for 'Hello'. She then acts as if the imaginary caller had offered a name as she seems to be echoing it, again in an intonation that is half questioning and half confirmation. After a slight pause she says, 'Yes, hello'. This second 'hello' now represents an acknowledgement of the pretend caller, and a recognition of a relationship which can then allow the call to proceed.

These elements are highly ritualised but they are functional. Just how taken for granted they are, and how important is their function, is usually perceived only when someone does not use the rituals. If a call is made and the receiver says nothing, the caller is rather taken aback, is forced into finding an alternative response and is at a disadvantage in the conversation. We expect people to respond in typical ways and these ways ease the transition from the silence of no call to the substantive dialogue of a conversation. They are necessary because unlike face-to-face conversation, callers cannot see each other and other ways of establishing relationships are not available.

Pam, then, has a content which proceeds very much as if a real conversationalist is on the other end. Pam responds to things said with an affirmative acknowledgement 'Yes' and 'OK. Yes' and plays an active role in developing and sustaining the conversation with a question. She has no trouble drawing the call to a close:

I [won't/will phone] tomorrow, Bye bye.

In addition to these structural elements, Pam also leaves pauses between her utterances. She understands the need for a space, although that does not in itself tell us that she knows what should go there.

Pam's talk shows us that she has made a complete short call and displayed a competence valued in being, and necessary to becoming, a fully telelphonic communicative member of society.

Where has this knowledge come from? We cannot be sure, but she may well have taken part in phone calls to grandparents and other relatives, and she may have spent many hours overhearing the typical segments of one side of telephone conversations. The one-sidedness is significant and will be addressed below.

There is one other aspect which is fairly fundamental to telephone conversation and that is identifying oneself as a caller. While, as can be seen above, these children frequently identified the person to whom they were pretending to talk, they hardly ever identified themselves; it was a very rare occurrence. There are a number of possible reasons for this. It may be because to the child, the person doing the calling is self-evident; thus it may be a failure to perceive the needs of the other person. It may be that children are most used to participating in real telephone calls in which they have already been identified. When parents say things like, 'Come and talk to grandma now', self-identification becomes redundant. This may be linked to only having experiences of real telephone calls which are always to people who are well known. Which ever it is, these young children clearly did not see a need to explicitly reveal themselves to the other callers.

While the context for developing a relatively complete telephone conversation was not always appropriate, it was nevertheless clear that when they wanted to, most of these young children could attain a useful degree of competence in using the underlying rules of telephone dialogue.

The person on the other end

One of the earliest learning tasks for an emergent telephone conversationalist is to understand that there is a person on the other end of the line. To some extent this must emerge through experience of participating in telephone conversations. However, the talk that surrounds telephone calls in homes probably also supplies important information about the other person. Callers will often tell other family members that they are going to call someone, and will often relate details of incoming calls and identify the caller. Thus the communicative nature of telephone calls is signalled by parents and other family members.

When many of the children's pretend calls are heard they seem totally realistic. Many, if simply seen as transcriptions, would be taken for real calls. The children often seem to posses a very rich range of competencies. However, what is heard is only ever one side of a conversation and it is as single-sided calls that they seem realistic. Research evidence, as well as personal experience, suggests that when children of this age actually have real telephone conversations they are often very passive, await questioning, and have difficulties in ending conversations. Working with an imagined other clearly seems easier than working with an actual other. Mininni (1985) has suggested that telephone conversations, whether in play or in reality, are valuable for the development of a young child's mental conception of another person and suggests that for pre-schoolers pretend telephone conversations might be better than actual telephone conversations in the 'training of a child's symbolic capacities'. This is, presumably, partly because pretend calls offer considerable practice in the mental evoking of another person.

However, it is to some extent an idealised person, who is always under the control of the imaginer. Very young children's real telephone calls are often made at the instigation of parents and usually involve speaking to adults. It is not surprising that in such circumstances young children often act in ways that make them look less than competent. The overall situation is under the control of adults (children are often told to 'come and speak to grandma'), and simply speaking to an adult at all probably places the child in a relationship in which she or he is less powerful. When the cognitive burden of using conversation outside of the child's normal face-to-face experience is added to this, then it should not be surprising that children exhibit what looks like greater competence in the pretend telephone event.

However, some questions need to be addressed in relation to this issue. What do children think they are doing when they engage in a pretend call? Do they actually imagine somebody on the other end of the phone talking to them? Are the children holding an imagined conversation or are they simply imitating an often-heard pattern; after all, as suggested above, what children will probably have experienced many times is one side of a conversation. When a parent makes or receives a telephone call the child usually witnesses only one half of the conversation. Such a pattern could be imitated and sound totally realistic. However,

41

as soon as the child is faced with a real person on the other end, an imitated pattern cannot unfold exactly as the overheard pieces; the child has to face the fact that the other speaker intervenes in ways which disrupt the pattern.

It may be possible to explore this issue through an examination of the pretend calls which were clearly marked as being to another person. Even in the very basic structure of the telephone call presented above, Pam seems to show the first traces of evoking an imaginary interlocutor in her awareness of turn taking, by her leaving pauses in her pretend dialogue. It is of course possible, as indicated above, that children doing this have no notion at all of another person and are simply imitating the pauses overheard when listening to telephone conversations at home. However, those calls which are more complex than Pam's seem to suggest some flexibility which is more than just simple imitation.

Many of the children in our study created clear identities for the 'person at the other end'. In fact sixty-one per cent of the calls featured such an identity: either a clearly distinguishable person or somebody with a clear function, such as somebody answering the phone 'for Goldilocks'. Such identities may have featured in more of the events but have not been marked in the talk, remaining imagined in the head of the child. Some identifications were declared to another person prior to the call: 'I'm going to ring my nana', or to another person during a call: 'I'm ringing my nana'.

The identification of the other person necessitates the formation of a relationship with that other person. No real conversation is ever neutral. Each speaker in a conversation reveals their relationship with the other through their speech. This is as true for pretend calls as it is for real calls. Pretend calls are not simply examples of a particular language skill; they richly illustrate children's relationships with other people in their world, and offer insight into a set of values, beliefs and attitudes. When children pretend to call their parents, the police, Goldilocks and so on, they set themselves up in a relationship to these people. These relationships exist in a zone between the knowledge they have about their real relationships with others and the relationships they can express through their imagination. In different 'conversations' these relationships will vary and it is through this variation, one might call it the creative element, that children surely move way beyond the limitations of imitation.

The most popular identification for these imaginary interlocutors (we cannot call them answerers since the 'conversations' sometimes indicated that the child was responding to, rather than initiating, a call) were the members of the children's immediate society: their family, grandparents, friends, teachers and caregivers, whether in or outside the nursery. In the pretend calls we recorded that the girls were more likely to call their mothers, while boys would call equally either mothers or fathers. For both sexes, though, the calls to mothers tended to be more detailed.

Some conversations with mothers and family members featured children apparently listening to exhortations and instructions, and the children displayed various reactions such as enthusiasm, assent or boredom, often by subtle variations in intonation alone. In the following conversation Ricky seems happy to adopt a relatively passive role, although the intonation of his responses reveals that one 'Yes Mum' can have a very different function from another one. It may be quite inaccurate to simply typify these responses as passive; through such back-channeling one speaker reassures the other of continuing interest and attention. (In this and most transcripts we indicated pauses or intonation shifts by moving to a new line.)

> Hiya Mum, Mum.
> Yes.
> Yes.
> Yes Mum.
> Yes Mum.
> Yes Mum.
> Yes.
> Yes Mum.
> Yes.
> Yes Mum.
> Yes.
> Oh yes Mum.
> Yes, yes.
> Yes Mum.
> Yes.
> Yes Mum.
> Yeh, yeh Mum.
> Yeh, yeh, bye.
> Bye Mum, bye bye, bye.

On the other hand, some children moved during a conversation from passivity to a more active role, as did Ryan:

(Ryan lifts receiver.)
Hello
(Pause.)
Hello Granny, Gran.
(Pause.)
Um.
(Pause.)
Yes.
(Pause.)
Uhh *(he laughs)*
You've crashed the car, oh.
(Pause.)
I'll be round in a minute.
(Pause.)
Yes, bye.
(Ryan puts receiver down.)

Other children gave instructions, very often to do with real-life matters such as telling people which sweets to buy. Watching the video recordings it was easy to believe that calls were genuine. For example, take Esme (with adult present outside hut):

(Esme speaks to adult:)
I've got to phone me Nanna up before she goes home.
(Picks up receiver. Dials and says to adult:)
What time is it?
(Adult replying to Esme says, 'Ten past one'.)
(Esme speaks into telephone:)
Hello....[a few words which were untranscribable]...what time, what time are you coming Nana to pick me up?
Four o'clock.
Right, Goodbye.
(Replaces receiver.)

In each of the three above conversations, the child creates a clearly identified person at the start of the call (although in the third example we know this initially only through the aside to the adult). The shift in relationship between the child and the imagined other across these three calls suggests a degree of spontaneity and control that seems beyond simple imitation.

Given the location in which the telephone was placed, it is not surprising that many of the phone calls were embedded in the surrounding socio-dramatic play. Calls often concerned Goldilocks and the three bears. It was an interesting contrast with the 'family and friends' calls that hardly anyone actually ever 'called' Goldilocks. An exception was Kim, although she did not actually manage to speak to Goldilocks:

> Hello, is that Goldilocks?
> Yes.
> Is she poorly?
> Pardon?
> Right, see you, bye.
> Right.
> Pardon?
> Right, see you, bye.
> Right, see you.

Usually they would telephone somebody and talk to them about Goldilocks or the bears. Here is an extract from a call made by Mike and Claire:

Mike	*(speaking into telephone)* ... and the bears are asleep right, do you know what, Goldilocks has been in our beds and the four bears, and do you know what, she ate the porridge and she ate ... she broke the chairs and she's still in bed ... (untranscribable)
Mike	*(Handing over the telephone to Claire)* Now you.
Claire	*(Speaking into telephone)* Hello, is the police there for me?
	Oh, good boy.
	(Speaks into telephone) Goldilocks has been pinching our beds and our (untranscribable). Will you ... would you come and steal her and eat her and chop her ... and chop her up. And chop her for us to eat.
	Good ... Bye bye.
Mike	*(Leaving hut)* I'll look for Goldilocks.

45

Despite the relatively short nature of many of the calls it seems reasonable to suggest that all these children go some way to creating a persona for the imagined interlocutor. Each assigns a distinct role to the imagined conversational partner and does so dramatically – the role is revealed rather than told; it has to be inferred from the way each child uses turns and moves within the exchange. Ricky assigns to Mum a perhaps all too familiar role of someone who talks at him incessantly, allows him spaces only for minimal responses and who seems happy that he simply listens and agrees. The intonational variety of his minimal responses expresses his sense of the frustrating constraints of his role as determined by the persona and power talk of the 'other' whose words we never hear.

Ryan lifts the receiver to hear Gran's familiar voice and appears to assume readily that the interaction will consist of the usual pleasantries associated with chats to Gran. Accordingly he settles himself down as the listener, back channelling warmly until suddenly Gran delivers a piece of news so disturbing that he must shift to a different role. At this point he uses a quite different, more proactive and decisive register appropriate to an emergency. His role as telephone conversationalist can be seen to be dramatically constructed by the role he implicitly assigns to Gran.

Kim too has to cope with unexpected events, for when she tries to ring Goldilocks she finds herself talking to some unidentifiable answerer who speaks on behalf of Goldilocks and who appears to insist on continuing to talk to Kim as she tries to end the conversation.

All the above children use the telephone as a private stage on which to enact a tiny but complete scene. The scene is constructed by a truncated text: all we are given are the children's words as they improvise small but eloquent turns in alternation with another imagined person who silently utters a more powerful text which contains unexpected events, news or respondents. Paradoxically, each child constructs the other speakers' role; it is the child's minimal text which reveals the interlocking second and often more powerful and interesting text.

Only Esme, as caller, is in full control as she uses the telephone to do one of those briefly functional arrangement-checking tasks; something for which the telephone is an ideal tool.

The rest of the children set themselves more demanding tasks, despite the fact that they cast themselves in the reactive rather than the proactive role.

Strategic use of language

One of the ways of showing children's strengths as telephone users is to look at their skills in varying their use of language for different situations. When we examined different types of calls we can see that not only did those types require specific uses of language, but that the children were able to supply it. One distinct group of events was the 'emergency' calls, which were a popular theme for many children.   The calls were usually stimulated by the surrounding socio-dramatic play.   Twenty-four calls were made to either the police, fire brigade or doctor to deal with a crisis. So in what ways did these calls show a specific use of language?   One important feature is the structure of the call. See for example Anna's call:

> **Anna**   Doctor come round tomorrow 'cos someone's
> poorly. It's teddy bear poorly so come round.

One third of the emergency calls followed this pattern: giving an explicit instruction in an imperative form 'Doctor come round tomorrow', closely accompanied by a relevant justification. Even when the instruction is not so explicit, the goal of the call was still often to demand appropriate action, as in Nina's call:

> **Nina**   Hello Doctor, don't forget. It's about Lincoln, he
> was resting on the bed, but he was [untranscribable]
> by a man and now he's dead.

Mike and Claire similarly make a sequence of calls attempting to telephone the police, but with limited success owing to wrong numbers and other problems.   However, as we have already seen, when Claire does 'succeed in getting through' she uses a request form but still supplies the police with a justification, here presented in reverse order as the extract shows:

> **Claire**   Goldilocks has been pinching our beds and our
> [untranscribable]. Will you...would you come and
> steal her and eat her and chop her...and chop her
> up and chop her for us to eat.
> Good. Bye bye.

Another feature of this specific use of language is displayed in the children's assertive style. This is necessitated in the making of emergency calls, which are therefore characterised by the use of requests and imperatives. Such features are characteristic of situations where time is short and urgent action is needed. The children, at a very young age, are able to use some of the essential features of the register of emergency calls.

The emergency calls afford the children the opportunity to display adult-type responsibilities and capabilities which their junior status in society would usually deny them. This is indicated not just in the content of the calls themselves but also in the surrounding speech. For example, prior to one call Laura announces 'You aren't ringing. I'll ring the police about there's a fire here.' In the course of Mike and Claire's play about the police and Goldilocks, part of which is given in the extract above, Mike several times says manfully, 'Don't cry, I ring the cop shop.'

There is an obvious deficiency in the children's emergency calls when compared with adult language in actual circumstances. The normal demands of emergency calls: dialling 999, speaking first to the operator and giving one's name and location, are always omitted by the children. We can surmise that for all children's fondness for making this type of call they are unlikely to have witnessed them in real life. More probably, their knowledge is picked up from such sources as television programmes, especially cartoons and soaps, where such realistic details may well have been omitted in the swift pace of the action.

The popularity of emergency calls, then, is probably not coincidental. They are dramatic, very active, appear to get things done and are fun. They demand a certain clear-cut register, central features of which have been grasped by the children. Finally they make the children feel important and capable. It therefore seems not unreasonable to suggest that they are beneficial in developing children's confidence in their oral skills.

It might perhaps be suggested that the features picked out above as being characteristic to emergency calls are in fact more ubiquitous. Certainly there are other calls which feature instructions, such as the small number to caregivers telling them to buy sweets! But the claim that the children do show differences in language strategy can be supported by comparing the emergency calls with two other types of call. Firstly, we shall use 'supplier' calls and secondly we shall show how one child, Gemma, varies her register in contrasting situations.

Telephoning a 'supplier' with an order for goods or services was a far less popular activity than telephoning mothers, relatives, caregivers, or friends, or the emergency calls. It is, however, another good example of the strategic use of language in a different social situation.

There were four calls of this type. In one Tina calls 'Minnie' to mend broken cups and afterwards explains, 'He was a mender'. In the other three calls there is, at least, a three-way conversation involved in the call (if we include the imaginary order-taker at the other end!).

For example, here is an extract from within an extended play episode between Andrew and Gail concerning the ordering of fruit:

(Gail picks up receiver.)
Gail: Do you want a hundred apples?
Andrew: Yes.
Gail dials.
Gail: *(into phone)* Hiya. A hundred apples.
(Pause.)
Gail: *(to Andrew)* A hundred oranges?
Andrew: Yes.
Gail: *(into phone)* A hundred oranges.
Gail: *(to Andrew)* A hundred pears?
Andrew: Yes.
Gail: *(into phone)* A hundred pears please.

It can be seen that Gail has grasped the nature of an order for goods in that, as in all the supplier calls, she allows the imaginary hearer time as if to take down the order. She is not afraid to use the kind of repetition that would probably be boring for her telephone partner in the context of a social call. Further, she is conscious of the need for the order to have been originated somehow – in this case with Andrew.

Esme on a separate occasion writes a list of wanted goods, having got 'the man' on the phone. She understandably appears to find the mechanics of writing the list and having the man hanging on meanwhile rather too much to deal with and abandons the call without succeeding in achieving a clear telephone order. Nevertheless, we can sympathise with her dilemma and see that these callers are attempting a problem-solving strategy and displaying a degree of competence in the use of this particular register.

We can now return to Gail in pursuit of our argument that the strategic use of language can be evidenced by two different calls by the same child. In one call, part of which was given above, Gail is clearly in charge of the process of making the fruit order. She is assertive as befits her position. Earlier that morning she had made a very different pretence call to her mother:

> *(Gail picks up receiver and dials.)*
> Hiya Mum.
> *(Pause.)*
> Yes Mum.
> *(Pause.)*
> Yes.
> *(Pause.)*
> Yes I am in the house.
> *(Pause.)*
> Yes.
> *(Pause.)*
> Yes.
> *(Pause.)*
> Don't do that.
> *(Angry groan.)*
> No, I'm in the three bears' house.
> *(Pause.)*
> No, stop it.
> *(Ends call).*

In this call Gail has shown the preference for expressing responses, often monosyllabically, that typified some of the children's pretend conversations with their mothers (as discussed above.) It would be a mistake to say that this call is truly more passive than the first; that there is some degree of imagining the mother's speech is indicated by the angry groan and use of 'no' which Gail uses after her earlier agreement. But it is clear that the pattern of chiefly making responses, which Gail shows when pretending to call her mother, is not the case when she is making an order to a supplier. In the supplier situation it would be an inappropriate language strategy in real life; to mothers it might be more likely and appropriate.

It would seem then that children's pretend telephone conversations reveal them as flexible and strategic telephone users. They have a repertoire of language skills and abilities from which can be selected appropriate moves in a variety of situations.

Conclusion

Earlier on in this chapter we questioned the reason for having telephones in schools. We asked 'Do they have an educational significance beyond being just another prop in the play area?' and 'Do they have any more status than the small pots and pans in the home corner?' Our answer to these questions has to be 'yes' for a number of reasons.

- *They offer opportunities for the development of a fundamental human competence.* Telephone conversations challenge conventional face-to-face conversational strategies. They demand subtle linguistic and cognitive moves which extend a child's ability to communicate with other people. As can be seen from the extracts included in this chapter, even very young children are exploring the communicative demands of this channel and are developing knowledge and strategies which are highly effective.

- *They generate opportunities for teachers to understand children's linguistic competence in wider contexts.* All teachers of young children will have heard children making pretend telephone calls. Their charm and interest often hides the powerful intellectual and linguistic moves being made by the children. Closer listening will help teachers to understand how individual children are developing complex language abilities, and will enable them to monitor the children's language in a variety of imagined situations that extend beyond many of the other opportunities available in classrooms. While in other kinds of socio-dramatic play children take on different roles, in telephone conversations they take on the control of two roles at the same time; a complex and demanding exercise.

- *They create chances for children to practise being in control of many different aspects of life.* We have shown that using the telephone for imagined conversations enables a range of roles to be enacted, but perhaps more powerfully, allows children to construct other people's roles without actual people interfering to behave differently and mess up the conversation. In these roles children can be 'authority' or can react towards authority in different ways. When they order goods or demand emergency services they challenge the world to react in response to their behaviour. Telephone play, like other kinds of play, allows children to try out a range of roles that are often denied them. What the pretend telephone behaviours show is that even the youngest children have developed skills which make a solid contribution to their ability to act powerfully upon the world.

In summary then, by listening to a young child's play telephone conversations a teacher or other adult can learn about the child's developing ability to control his or her use of language in special, but very important and complex communicative situations. At least as important is the opportunity to observe the child's enactment and representation of aspects of his or her social and material world. In calling an imagined person, a child can extend the limits of his or her communicative abilities and imagined social responsibilities in the safe, generally supportive context of pretence play.

Even as a toy, a telephone is a powerful instrument; it has magic power to summon anyone, to offer access to any individual or any context; and to offer personal contact with any agency, service or situation, real or fantastic, actual or imagined. In learning to use the telephone a child is learning to interact effectively through language with a world of diverse but particular circumstances.

Pretend telephone calls make possible many things, but Elise has clearly got her priorities sorted out.

Andrew	What would you like?
Elise	I would like a fortune.
Andrew	*(says into phone)* Have you got, have you got a fortune? Elise wants a fortune.

References

Bjelic, Dusan (1987) On hanging up in telephone conversation, *Semiotica,* Vol. 67 (3–4) 195–210.

Bordeaux, M. A. and Willbrand, M. L. (1987) Pragmatic development in children's telephone discourse, *Discourse Processes,* Vol. 10 (3) 253–366.

Garvey, C. and Berndt, S. (1975) *The organisation of pretend play.* Revised version of paper given at Annual Convention of American Psychological Association.

Holmes, Janet (1981) 'Hello–goodbye: an analysis of children's telephone conversations', *Semiotica,* Vol. 37 (1–2) 91–107.

Mininni, G. (1985) 'The ontogenesis of telephone interaction' *Rassegna Italiana di Linguistica Applicata,* Vol. 17 (2–3) 187–197.

Warren, Amye and Tate, C. (1992) Egocentrism in children's telephone conversations in Diaz, R. and Berk, L. *Private speech: from social interaction to self-regulation.* Hillsdale, NJ: LEA.

4

Children's conceptions of imaginative play revealed in their oral stories

Carol Fox

This chapter looks at the invented oral stories of young children in order to answer the following questions:

- How is play represented in the stories?

- Do the young story tellers reveal any explicit awareness of what play is?

- What can we learn about children's conceptions of play from their imaginative story material?

- What implications does this have for understanding cognitive development?

The story data referred to in this chapter are 200 oral invented stories narrated spontaneously by five pre-school children, and tape-recorded by the children's parents. Although these data were collected in the early 1980s, and although I have written about them extensively elsewhere (Fox 1993), they comprise approximately 49,000 words of narrative and remain a rich bank of potential evidence for many aspects of children's cognitive and linguistic development.

A survey of the content of the 200 stories immediately shows that there are remarkably few references to play in them. On the rare occasions when play is referred to we hear that the characters 'played' but the play itself is not described. Toys are sometimes mentioned and characters sometimes play with them, but most typically none of the details is given. When Jimmy tells a story about his teddy-bears coming to life (a favourite fantasy in children's invented stories and in stories written for children) the focus of the story is on what the magical teddies can do, not on what the children who play with them do imaginatively to make them more 'real' and lifelike. When Josh tells a story in which Julie buys a doll, David buys a mechanical digger, and the fictional Josh buys 'the biggest bomb in the world' the subsequent narrative tells of the damage Josh is able to do with his bomb. There is no description of how the characters actually played with their toys. Five-year-old Sundari, however, refers more often to play. In one story a boy called Cletcher goes to the fair and has several rides. Sundari's narration leaves us in no doubt as to the pleasure of this kind of play:

> ... and also they went on some swings
> they loved to go on swings
> they went as high and low and high and low and high and low ...

This is narrated very expressively indeed with very strong rising and falling intonation on the 'high and low' repetitions. While the children successfully communicate the satisfaction of playing with apparatus, objects and toys, they do not give descriptions of the sort of activity they themselves are engaged in as they tell their stories, the mental creation of an imaginary world. However, there is one remarkable story by Sundari in which this does happen.

The story is Sundari's 'story 12', told when she was about five-and-a-half years old. In my book *At The Very Edge Of The Forest* (1993) I have analysed this story very extensively, showing how it employs a startlingly high number of the variations in tense, mood, and voice identified by Genette in *Narrative Discourse* (1972). Sundari's story is not only remarkably complex in terms of the subtleties of its chronologies, points of view, and types of narrating, but it is extraordinary in other ways. It has a highly developed sense of poetic rhythm, uses words with originality and sensitivity, and is syntactically very advanced. The story tells of a little girl, Laura, who initially loses her way when playing on the beach with her dolls. In an abrupt change of scene in the middle of the story, Sundari's character has her favourite necklace stolen by another girl at school. After this Laura does not go to school any more, but stays alone on the beach playing with her dolls. Eventually she returns home, and the story ends in a magnificent passage in which Laura and her dolls listen to the West wind. At this point it is worth quoting Sundari's descriptions of Laura playing (long spaces in the transcription represent pauses in the telling of the story):

> She liked doing things   playing about at the beach on sunny days when cool wind was blowing   making sand castles playing with her little necklace with some people on it   and some little raindrops falling from the people   and bags on it what the teddy bears were in what the people were holding   and she had little teddy bear earrings   she had lots of things   and she mostly played with her dolls   made sand castles for them and little beach houses   and she did lots of things loads of things ...

A little further on in her story Sundari changes the scene to a day in school:

> ... and she had loads of things she had to do at school   one day a girl called Meg said 'Why can't I wear that necklace? Why does Laura have to wear it all the time?' And she told the teacher and the teacher said 'Laura take your necklace off'   but Laura didn't know where she put it   it was her best necklace she was wearing and the teddy bears in the bags and the people on with the raindrops   she was crying in the playground but when she got in the class she knew where her necklace was   when the teacher wasn't looking she quickly took it off and put it in her pocket and as soon as it was home time   when it was when she got a partner   she put the necklace back on ...

Now Sundari returns to playing on the beach:

> ... she played and played in the seaside playing with her dolls   making little roads and houses for them to go in   little sandpies for them to eat   and little cool rivers for them to wash and drink cups full of the drink from the little river for the dolls that really could drink 'cos most of them – but the other dolls could really eat   so could the ones who could really drink – and to dolls that could really eat and drink (what all of them – and)   all little things could fit down their little – little mouths and when they wanted to wee   they went to the toilet which was really a little potty made out of paper   and they got on it and a drink came out by holding their clothes ...

Story 12 moves from Laura's imaginative solitary play to her interaction with other characters and back again to her solitary play. In other words, it depicts a movement from an inner world to an outer one, and then back to the inner one. The change from one kind of experience to the other is marked by the storyteller in several ways. The pace of the storytelling and the duration of the actions is slow in Sundari's 'inner world' passages. She often uses what Genette calls iterative frequency, that is the kind of story time in which things would happen typically and habitually rather than the kind of story time in which specific things happen only once. There is also a lyrical quality in the way in which Sundari's narrator describes things in the 'inner world' passages, which contrasts with the sharp, dramatic dialogue she uses for Laura's day at school. This marking of a change from imagining to real experience is parallel to the conventions of many picture story books for young children.

Books such as John Burningham's *Come Away From The Water, Shirley* (1977) juxtapose on the left and right pages of the text the two different worlds inhabited by the main character. In Burningham's story dull pastel colours are used to depict the boring world of Shirley's parents, sitting on the beach in deckchairs with their flasks and newspapers. On the opposite pages the imaginary world of pirates, shipwrecks, islands, buried treasure, and sunsets is represented by the vivid colours of films, paintings, and some dreams. Not all children understand that Shirley is imagining this secondary, more vivid world. Children up to the age of eight or nine sometimes try to explain how it is possible for Shirley to do all these exciting actions without her parents noticing what is going on. They even observe that we don't have pirates any more but are at a loss to explain the contradiction in the two types of narrative time, that of the 'real' present and that of some fictional bygone era.

In some books, for example, the Shirley stories, Sendak's *Where The Wild Things Are* (1967), Mckee's *Not Now Bernard* (1980) or Briggs' *The Snowman* (1978), and many others like them, the authors do not make explicit the movement from a realistic world to an imaginary one. Instead, the change is connoted by the techniques of the artwork. Children must work out for themselves what is *really* going on when they are ready to understand. As Meek (1988) has pointed out, the act of reading stories itself involves just

57

such a change from an outer to an inner world, so children who have heard and read a lot of stories are likely to become aware of this kind of mental picturing sooner. Meek's point is that the very act of imagination involved in interpreting a story has become a major topic of many modern children's books. Dream narratives of the kind where the dreamer awakes at the end of the story to return to the real world – *The Wizard Of Oz* and *Alice In Wonderland* are two classic examples – are rather different, in that the narrator in such stories provides the reader with a rational explanation for the fantasy material – it was all a dream.

In dreams our imaginings, however fantastical, are involuntary. We have no control over summoning them into being. In our daydreams and stories, however, we have the chance to be more aware of our own mental activity. Dorothy and Alice awake from their dreamworlds but we do not imagine that Shirley and Max are asleep when visiting the treasure island or the land of the wild things. Even though this distinction can be made it is unusual for children's stories, either those written for them or those invented by them, to make the act of imagining explicit. When the teddy bears and monsters of Jimmy's invented oral story come to life and have a battle, the imaginative activity which brought them into being is implicit, represented as a form of magic. The magical transformation of one thing into another is so common in children's literature that it can be safely taken for granted as understood; the convention is well established.

All of this makes Sundari's story 12 very unusual. Story 12 is a reflection not only of Sundari herself at play in her storytelling, revealing her implicit knowledge of what it is to construct a world imaginatively, it is also a reflection of Sundari's explicit knowledge of play, since she is consciously representing an imagined world in which her characters play imaginatively.

Vygotsky (1978) calls imaginative play a second-order symbolism. He says the first-order symbolism is oral language itself. He describes a process by which the child moves from using gestures and actions to represent things symbolically, to making early scribbles and primitive drawings stand in for their meanings, and later to using writing to represent words and speech – hence a second-order symbolism; the writing represents oral language which, in turn, represents elements in the world. How does Sundari's story fit into this? Is oral storytelling a first-order or second-order symbolism? Sundari clearly uses a first-order symbol system to tell her stories – oral language. But, is using those words to create an imaginary world an example of second-order symbolism? In some ways it is. She is using language not to represent real everyday experience but to transform that experience into something else – something new. Gestures and actions are not part of this representation in words, though Sundari does use the range of intonational features of spoken language. Not only is Sundari's created world dependent on words alone (as in writing) but it employs conventions and structures which do not belong to interactive conversation. Sundari has no face-to-face audience for her story, only the tape-recorder. Therefore, as in writing, her addressee is removed in both time and place. It is possible that the very act of telling her stories alone with the tape-recorder heightens Sundari's awareness of what she is doing.

Furthermore, Sundari's story and narrative conventions, as well as several ideas and motifs, are taken from books she has heard read aloud. Joan Aitken's story *A Necklace Of Raindrops* (1968) is a very important source for Sundari's narrative. Her character Laura, the scene at school where a girl called Meg steals Laura's necklace, and the idea of the powerful winds, are all taken directly from the Aitken story. (Incidentally Aitken's book is not a picture book; Sundari would have had to listen to the story and picture its scenes for herself.) In spite of drawing on this source material Sundari transforms it into something new of her own. The question of symbolic order becomes more complicated when Sundari invents a character who plays imaginatively and when she describes what that character does to invent a world for her dolls. The dolls' invented world is embedded within Sundari's created world of the story which in its turn is embedded within Sundari's competence for linguistic representation. One could imagine the embeddings continuing forever – Sundari creates Laura who in turn creates dolls who are 'real' who in their turn invent dolls for themselves to play with and so on.

What is the process of Laura's play with her dolls? Laura tries to bring her dolls to life by imitating eating, drinking, and urinating in the most realistic way she can. Does the storyteller invoke magic to bring this about? Does Laura 'cheat' by having a magic doll like the teddy bears of Jimmy's stories? No. The dolls have orifices, and in this respect are like real people, but, in spite of some linguistic confusion, we are in no doubt that Laura's dolls are only dolls, and that their food and drink must be represented by sand and water. The dolls do not speak or get up and take a walk. Unlike Jimmy's teddy bears they do not come to life. Sundari's character Laura 'pretends' that they are real. With the props around her on the beach she makes them eat and drink and hold their clothes so that they can take a pretend pee.

My point here is not that it is unusual for five-year-olds to play in this way but that on the contrary, it is extremely common for them to do so, and Sundari's character is directly parallel to Vygotsky's example of little girls pretend-playing mothers. But, it is unusual for children to narrate stories which include such explicit descriptions of this sort of play. Once a child has achieved such a narration her imaginative activity is no longer merely spontaneous and unrehearsed; it now becomes a focus for reflection. She can now think about her own thinking and reflect on the capacity of her own mind to have ideas and bring things into being. I shall discuss the cognitive implications of this a little later. Before leaving story 12 I want to look at some other aspects of the passages which describe Laura's playing.

I have already touched upon the ways in which these passages employ quite sophisticated chronologies, and variations in duration and frequency (Genette's terms for changes of pace in the telling and for differences in the kind of past time in which things occurred). If these are interesting passages from the point of view of the technicalities of Sundari's storytelling skills, they are also interesting from the point of view of their emotional tone. Vygotsky argued that pleasure or desire should not be separated from our notion of what play is. From Sundari's lingering repetitions of rhythms and phrases in these passages, which in places are constructed like poems, we can see that she has learned how to use language both to express her character's pleasure in her imaginative play and to express her own pleasure in inventing that play with no other materials at her disposal than the words she uses to tell the story. The scene at the school, derived from Joan Aitken, is by contrast told in a plain and matter-of-fact way, mainly through the use of dialogue (some of it borrowed from the Aitken original).

School is thus represented as an environment where children do not have the opportunity for the kind of creative play Sundari describes in the rest of her story. Sundari's outer world is a mean place compared to her inner one.

What are the implications of this for cognition? There are several which ought to be considered now that pre-school and nursery education are coming under such scrutiny.

- Sundari shows a great awareness of the difference between the real and the fantastic – though we should not lose sight of the fact that *all* of this is fantastic since it is all embedded within a story Sundari is making up.

- Sundari knows that imaginative play involves ideas and mental activity on the part of the player. To transform her dolls into something more real she must be inventive and ingenious, making use of the materials that surround her on the beach.

- Sundari is aware that we do not need companions in order to play – we can invent them.

- Sundari is moving away from the use of magic and co-incidence as a plotting device and towards cause and effect and logical explanations for phenomena.

- Sundari is becoming explicitly aware of her own mental activity and is able to represent that awareness in language. This must give her much better control over her own mental processes.

- Sundari is able, in storytelling, to hold several degrees of embedded representation in her mind, and move freely from one to another. I have written elsewhere that Sundari's invention of herself as a narrator who addresses her unknown audience directly, is but her initial act of representation. The narrator then invents a character and the character, Laura in this case, goes on to reinvent her dolls as something more lifelike than they are. Sundari also invents her audience, who are not physically present, but must be imagined for some future occasion when they listen to her tape. All writing involves imagining an audience.

- Although such explicit representations of creative play are rare in stories by and for children, should we regard Sundari's accomplishment as something advanced and special, or is it likely to be part of all children's imaginative competency? Do children know what they are doing when they play creatively? I am inclined to think that they do. Children in their pretend play move in and out of role all the time. When they break the play and move out of role it is often to plan and set up the conditions for the next part of the act. Though they do not 'break' the play lightly, making it clear that the fun of it is to stay in role, nevertheless their excursions from their unwritten scripts into real life usually reflect a very explicit awareness of what they are doing (Evershed, 1995).

- This explicit awareness will of course be more evident in children who play imaginatively, or read, or storytell, or write a lot. Children's awareness of their own imaginations can only come from the frequent practice of them. This is often not understood by curriculum makers and educationists. The sort of verbal fantasy play that Sundari is so good at is very like reading and writing. It is solitary. Words have to be uttered for audiences who are not physically present. Things have to be explained in ways comprehensible to those who have, for interpretation, to rely on only the words.

New proposals for nursery education in the UK appear to be importing into four-year-olds' school experiences activities that were previously left until children were five or older. What is more, many four-year-olds are now in full-time education alongside five-year-olds. The planners of curricula for young children need to recognise, as Vygotsky did, the links between early symbolic play and later mental development, especially in the realms of abstract thinking and literacy learning. Sundari's story arises from her experience of hearing a story read aloud – not any old story, but a favourite story. We can deduce this from the way she remembers some of Joan Aitken's phrases so accurately. Sundari's story also prepares her very well for writing, where she will require the same mental operations she has performed in her oral storytelling. Play of the kind Sundari describes is common coin – almost all children do it to a greater or lesser degree. What education needs to do is harness that creative play, make scope for it, encourage it, and help children to reflect on it and develop it.

References

Aitken, J. (1968) *A Necklace Of Raindrops.* London: Jonathan Cape.

Briggs, R. (1978) *The Snowman.* London: Hamish Hamilton.

Burningham, J. (1977) *Come Away From The Water, Shirley.* London: Jonathan Cape.

Evershed, J. (1995) The Expression of a Range of Discursive Roles and Positions in Young Children's Voluntary Pretend Play; University of Brighton, Unpublished PhD Thesis.

Fox, C. (1993) *At The Very Edge Of The Forest.* London: Cassell.

Genette, G. (1972) *Narrative Discourse* (Trans. 1980) Oxford: Basil Blackwell.

McKee, D. (1980) *Not Now Bernard:* London: Andersen Press.

Meek, M. (1988) *How Texts Teach What Readers Learn.* Stroud Glouc: Thimble Press.

Sendak, M. (1963) *Where the Wild Things Are.* London: The Bodley Head.

Vygotsky, L. (1978) *Mind In Society.* Cambridge, Mass.: Harvard University Press.

5

My mind is like a book that never ends

Geane Hanson

It's like sometimes, my imagination – sometimes when I am daydreaming it's like long – and I can keep on using my imagination and could keep on daydreaming for the rest of my life. And so it's kinda like a book, where you don't know what's gonna happen, except it never ends.

(Ellen, aged 7)

For the past several years I have been talking with children about their thinking lives while they engage in reading and writing in their classrooms. Like Ellen, other children implicitly understand the connection between reading, writing and literacy and how daydreaming and imagination support that process. Yet traditionally, it has often been tacitly assumed that daydreaming is building castles in the air and a waste of productive school time. With the growing recognition of the need for a more inclusive, comprehensive and intertextual view of learning in school, also comes the understanding that complex aspects of cognition, such as thinking, imagination and daydreaming are significant. Hence, educators might reconsider daydreaming as an aspect of children's thinking and imaginative lives which contributes to, rather than detracts from, their learning lives.

As a teacher and researcher it never ceases to amaze me how articulate children are regarding their thinking lives and mental processes. Not only are young children articulate, but they are generally eager to engage in conversation regarding what goes on in their minds while playing, reading, writing and problem solving. Their enlivened feedback often indicates they may even be flattered by the idea that someone, particularly an adult, really wants to know such personal aspects of their internal mental landscape at any given moment in time.

This chapter is concerned with children's inner lives as daydreamers. Through vignettes of real interactions, I would like to share some meta-cognitive insights of three young children (aged four to eight) regarding their mental processes.

Profiles of three daydreamers

Marie

Marie tells me she is four and will be five on Valentine's Day. She has a new baby sister and she also has two friends, named Marshada and Marboobie, who no one but she can see and talk to. Her parents explain that she has had these two imaginary friends since she first began talking and more recently has begun to mention that they plan to 'move away and live with their mom'

One day after school Marie and I walk to her house where she reads me some of her books. The only problem is, we are constantly interrupted; Marboobie is in the closet with no clothes on. Marshada is in there too, wearing only red shorts. Marie pokes her head into the closet door and hollers at them to be quiet and stop 'fooling around in there' as she pulls some clothes off hangers, asking them to 'please get dressed'. Marie returns from the closet and continues reading to me.

When the book is finished I ask her what her friends are doing in the closet. She tells me they are both very naughty and say a lot of bad words which she isn't permitted to repeat. Marie explains how the other day in the car Marshada hit her. Marie animates the event, 'Would you move and quit pushing me and get outta my way?' She goes on to explain that Marshada has a mom but she and Marboobie are staying with Marie and don't get to see their mom very often. However, their mom is coming today and she is due to arrive at the same time Marie's own mother returns home. She then tells me how the other night Marshada woke up her baby sister. Then, just as quickly, Marie hops up, dances down the hall and goes outside to play with the old dog, whom she explains can no longer 'see a thing'.

Four-year-old Marie appears to blend her daydreams and imaginative ponderings directly with her lived experience. For her, there is no problem with Marshada and Marboobie being in the closet with no clothes on. She is just as matter of fact about that as she is about her old dog loosing its eyesight. When I ask her about daydreaming she looks up at me a bit baffled and continues to sing me a story from her book. My question is not worth addressing; apparently such a notion does not have the same meaning for her as it obviously does for me. She is a functioning, practising daydreamer without need to categorise and make such meta-cognitive distinctions.

However, when I ask what Marboobie looks like, she goes into great detail describing her as big, having long red hair and a naughty side to her personality. In talking with very young children about daydreaming I find they demonstrate their inner life through outer expression, rather than reflect on it. She does not know what a daydream is as she is still too busy inhabiting her own. Marie is not unusual in this way; as Marie continues to grow so will the distinctions she makes regarding her inner world. Her rich inner resources will grow as she grows, reflecting the growing context of her internal and external experience in the world.

Ed

Ed is eight years old and goes to a 'whole language' school. We have been sitting on the rug listening to the teacher, Ms Lohse, read a story about a family from Cambodia who have just moved to America. Ed turns to tell me with great enthusiasm about the story he is writing now:

> I'm only on the second page – but 'cause I can't think of what to say and stuff, like the other characters – what they should say. But, so far it's about this: these two kids find a dummy and then they find this, it's like a round stone and then they have like Japanese writing on it.

I follow him to the table and our conversation continues as he looks for his writing folder to continue working on his story, which is titled 'The Cursed Dummie'.

Ed explains his approach to story writing, 'First I imagine what the beginning will be and then as I go on I imagine farther into the story.'   He likes putting his ideas on paper, ... 'so everybody can know them and stuff.'   Ed is a prolific writer who is known in the classroom community for his epic, 'to-be-continued' style of writing stories.   When he writes he explains, 'I think of them and then I get them, the ideas of what's going to happen and then I write it down.'   One of the techniques Ed uses in capturing the characteristics of the characters in his stories is to daydream they are there talking to him.   He explains:

> I like to daydream ... sometimes I daydream that I daydream
> up a character and then I daydream that he is like sitting right
> next to me and, he talks and does some and – then I know he
> does some stuff and so I know his chareristics. So I can put
> them into my story.

I ask Ed what these characters look like in his daydreams and he explains, 'They look like real people when I am daydreaming about one thing ... they usually look like cartoons when I am thinking, 'cause there is everything in it.'   When he is thinking of a story where there is a lot happening, the images in his mind are more cartoon-like. When he is daydreaming about a character and imagining a conversation between them, his images are more real. He reflects further on this process in writing by stating ' ... I daydream about – when I have pictures in my head, but all of it is still and then I put it into my imagination and it comes more real.'

When I inquire further as to the distinction he makes between daydreaming and imagination he explains that he usually 'imagines about books and stories', particularly when he is reading chapter books that don't have pictures in them.   He gives the example of the 'Goosebumps' series by R. L. Stine,   'They are supposed to be scary ... like at parts that weird stuff is happening, I usually think of what the weird stuff looks like in my head.' Daydreaming while reading allows him to stop and process what he is reading and as Ed poignantly reveals, ' ... 'cause I understand the story, so then I can go on.'

Ed reflects thoughtfully and capably on his inner world of mental images, thinking, imaginings and daydreams. He makes distinctions between the ways he thinks up ideas for writing that indicate a developed sense of awareness of his own thinking processes:

> I think daydreaming is funner than thinking – 'cause thinking has to like think of ideas and you have to think of the ideas, but once you get it you can daydream with your ideas and play like – and once you get the idea you can daydream and play around with it, so you can change it and see which one you like most.

Daydreaming is an activity that nourishes his thinking life, both inside and outside school. One day he was doing math, '... and I was daydreaming when we were doing that 'cause I thought it was boring.' Daydreaming at a time like that helps him keep engaged in the activity at hand, 'I tried it without doing it like that and I think it's really boring and I don't get it done as fast.' When I inquired about what he was doing and thinking when he occasionally daydreams during math, he explained:

> Like when we're doing stuff like take away numbers, like I daydream that one of the numbers turns into, like it still looks like a number, but it gets teeth and like eats the other numbers that we have to take away and then it goes back to its original form and then I have the answer.

Such mental evocation of action is strikingly reminiscent of the children in Hughes's (1986) study who imagined all kinds of unusual ways of representing mathematical operations.

According to Ed, daydreaming is fun anytime because 'You can think up stuff that's not real.' At home he sometimes daydreams about superheroes and pretends there are big meetings of the heroes he reads about and watches in cartoons. 'I am on the walls and I am... imagining that I am on a really tall building and I am on the very edge of it – walking – then I usually jump off and I am usually flying down.' When he goes out shopping with his family he sometimes escapes to the next isle of the grocery store and pretends to be a 'spy or something'. As far as Ed is concerned, daydreaming is more fun than playing outside, 'I think that playing, just playing outside like on playground equipment, isn't as fun as daydreaming, as playing at what you are daydreaming.'

Ellen

Ellen is seven years old and in the same multi-age, whole language classroom with Ed. She knew about my interest in daydreams and imagination and sought me out on several occasions to tell me about something she was reading, writing or thinking. She enjoys talking about her own mental processes and when she does her eyes often look as though she is trying to somehow see inside herself. One day Ellen and Mandy, a fellow classmate, were discussing what thinking was like for each of them. I happened to walk by the table while they were actively engaged in talk while writing their 'Cinderella' stories.   Ellen told Mandy her mind was like a book of ideas that never comes to an end. Mandy then followed with her own metaphor, stating that she thinks of her mind more like an attic where she can store all kinds of things and bring them out when she needs them.   Ellen and I continued talking about her 'Cinderella' story and the relationship of daydreaming and imagination in her own process of writing. Daydreaming sometimes gives her 'ideas' for her stories. She explains, 'I was thinking of, like what it looked like, that she was doing, that they were making her do. And I saw like the ashes all over her face and the tears on her clothes and everything.' Although in her mind such images and daydreams are 'more blurry, they're not as realistic'.

Ellen too makes distinctions between the role of daydreaming, imagination and thinking in her mental life. 'When you daydream you are off in another world, seeing things that you are not really, you know that you are not really there, but when you are pretending you are there, I think that is different.' For Ellen thinking and imagining are more like 'pretending you are there'. I probe this distinction further with her and she explains, 'Well, 'cause imagination you more pretend and when you are daydreaming, it's like you are just seeing the thing, and you're not pretending to be there or be that thing, the person.' In daydreams Ellen always 'sees and hears' things, but when she is thinking she explains, '...you don't always see it or hear it ... thinking is sorta boring for me.'

Ellen likes the feelings associated with time spent daydreaming and imagining:

I like it cause it's like going off somewhere that's not reality. Like, umm, 'cause sometimes I think that people need to get away from your real life and get into like a pretend life or another world, about where you just imagine or daydream about stuff ... if you are frustrated or if you are irritated and it's just like if somebody is bothering you, then you just start imagining about stuff and then you don't really know that they are bothering you.

According to her, it is 'mostly kids' who daydream and imagine because 'kids have more fun stuff to imagine about'. Ellen thinks this is because kids don't have 'as much work to do' as adults do. When she is daydreaming her mind is often so focused that she won't hear someone calling, '... if somebody calls me in for dinner I don't hear them – I don't know that they are there.' She goes on to explain that this also happens when she is reading a good book:

Sometimes it happens when I am reading. If I am reading a book about a mystery – it is like I am really there and not at home reading and my mom is calling me for dinner, or somebody is calling me to do something and I don't know that it's happening.

While Ellen reads she often sees pictures in her head. 'I like to see how they describe it in my head, in pictures . . . wherever it is, I see that place in my head or I see that person in my head.' For her, the writing and reading processes are different imaginatively because when she writes, ' ... like you are making it up as you go along and you know pretty much what is going to happen and in a book you don't know what is going to happen next.' Ellen explains daydreaming is more akin to reading, 'because when you are dreaming you don't know what's gonna happen in your dreams next.' Her metaphor for her own mind is also related to her literate life, '... it's kinda like a book where you don't know what's gonna happen except it never ends.'

Ellen became so interested in the notion of reflecting on her own thinking process that there was seldom a day when she would not initiate conversation with me about some further discovery she had pondered regarding her imaginative thinking life. On the very last day of school, she came running up to me on the playground and told me her family was going to go on a trip to Oregon the day after school finishes. She tells me that she has been spending a lot of time thinking about what it will be like. She likes to draw pictures of what she imagines the scenery will be like. Sometimes she draws people too, like her Grandma. She wishes her Grandma could go with them, but she died this year. With her face bathed in Arizona sunlight she closes her eyes and tells me how sad she felt when her Grandma died and how much she daydreamed about her during that time. 'Well, my Grandma died and I was like, umm. . . I pretended that I was like sometimes flying, like, or I was flying with her, or doing something like that.'

Discussion

Young children are very close to their inner worlds. In the case of Marie, she does not yet differentiate the inner and outer worlds in her thinking life. However, both Ed and Ellen are capable of making many distinctions regarding their inner mental activity, often pointing out nuances adults forget to consider. Ed and Ellen frequently point out the connections between literacy and daydreaming/imagination. Daydreaming nourishes their writing, their reading of story and their sense of self in the world. It is through their daydreams/imaginations they see Marboobie naked in the closet, become the characters in favourite books, meet with superheroes, spy on family members, reinvent Cinderella and make sense of events like the death of a dearly loved Grandmother. While reading, they cease to hear the outside world as they are suspended in the life of the story. Similarly, when they daydream they often forget to attend to what is happening around them, and may miss a call to dinner.

These children indicate that daydreaming is not building castles in the air. Rather it exists in the context of their lived experience of individual thinking lives. Ed and Ellen spend time daydreaming both in school and outside of school; daydreaming is valued. Often when talking to children from more traditional classrooms, daydreaming is appropriate everywhere but in school. Ed's and Ellen's experience of schooling includes their inner lives in their outer production. They are encouraged to talk to each other, relate to their own ideating, thinking, daydreaming and imaginative journeys as they make sense of, and construct meaning in, their literate lives. In other words, this kind of time-off task is valued. Therefore, both Ed and Ellen are enthusiastic rather than resistant to talk about what they do in their own minds.

Children are capable conversationalists, making meta-cognitive distinctions regarding the nuances of their own mental process and more complex functions. This means that we, as adults, can no longer assume that we know more about what is happening with children than the children themselves.

The challenge for teachers is to go deeper in the authentic understanding of both the inner and outer lives of children. It also requires building relationships of trust with children and entering into a dialogue about the more complex aspects of their thinking and imaginative lives. In other words, we must give children the opportunity to speak about their own minds, enlightening knowledge of their inner processes. Like language, daydreaming is a uniquely human activity. For educators, this implies reconsideration of its value, rather than assuming a tacitly negative view. All human beings daydream. Hence, it must have functional value for human existence.

As teachers' and researchers' understanding of the social dimension of children's lives increases, so it is important not to overlook the inner lives of children. Too often the assumption is made that children are unable to articulate the complex meta-cognitive that goes on inside their own minds. Adults sometimes assume knowledge about what is happening in the minds of children rather than gather explicit information gleaned through talking with children.

Ellen's metaphor for her mind being like 'a book that never ends', reveals that young children are capable of enlightening us about their inner thinking processes. However, the responsibility to ask, engage in dialogue, and provide a safe context for exploring such personal realms lies with us.

What does a glimpse through the window of children's inner thinking processes mean for classroom teachers of young children? I think it means valuing time spent 'off task', encouraging them to engage in conversation, giving them the time and space to integrate and understand what they encounter as learners, making knowledge their own as they daydream conversations with characters in books and nourish their ideas for stories.

Classrooms where teachers are careful kid-watchers and kid-listeners are places where reflection is supported and nourished, not admonished. These classrooms can be sanctuaries where children are given the gift of time to wade in the constant river of their own ideas and time to feel the never ending possibility of their imagination. Indeed, then the mind seems to be a place of limitless possibility, like Ellen's book where the story has no end.

> Who is the story teller? Of whom is the story told? What is there in the darkness to imagine into being? What is there to dream and to relate? What happens when I or anyone exert the force of language upon the unknown ... We are what we imagine. Our very existence consists in our imagination of ourselves. Our best destiny is to imagine at least completely who and what and that we are. The greatest tragedy that can befall us is to go unimagined.
>
> (Momaday, 1970, p.55)

References

Hughes, M. (1986) *Children and number*. London: Blackwell.
McLaughlin, D. (1994) Critical Literacy for Navajo and Other American Indian Learners *Journal of American Indian Education*, **5**, 47–60.
Momaday, M.S. (1970) The man made of words, in Assembly Presentation Conference. *Indian Voices*, (pp. 49–69). San Francisco: Indian Historic Press.

6

The alligator as narrator

Sue Freeman

Class 3 have a problem concerning an alligator narrating a story: a closed door, and on the other side an innocent child victim leaving a note for his father. How can the alligator, who is not present at that moment, have access to the contents of the note and maintain his status as the all-knowing narrator of the story they are recreating? A solution is found: a glass panel in the door, thin paper, felt tips and, one supposes, the ability of alligators to read back to front. All the children are satisfied; a logic born of their seven years of real-world experience impels their narrative to its next event.

We have returned to the classroom after our Friday library period. At the end of a week spent highlighting the mechanics of writing (capital letters and full stops, clear ascenders and descenders, unmixed upper and lower case letters) for the benefit of the twenty, soon to be assessed, children within the class, our Friday library period inevitably represents, both for the children and myself, a chance to relax, albeit in a literary environment. This could easily deteriorate into an opportunity for the children to squabble over the bean bags and the *Where's Wally* books, and for me to perform an undemanding administrative role as I chase up unreturned books. But instead, we share the bean bags and talk.

During their single term with me, we have discussed information on book covers; gender issues; anthropomorphism; fact books; re-reading favourite picture books; and what makes us want to go on reading a book. After a workshop with the author Anthony Browne we consider illustrators and authors, searching the shelves for books by those individuals like Anthony Browne who can fulfil both functions. We discuss why the size of books is so important to the children, why they are dissatisfied with reading 'little, thin, short books' and yearn for 'chapter books, big, fat books, books without any pictures.'

Over the weeks the talk turns from the format of books to aspects of the stories within them: openings and endings, favourite characters, motives, plot and the resolution of problems. Time well spent I reassure myself with an eye to the forthcoming assessment demands which require the children to 'demonstrate, in talking about stories and poems, that they are beginning to use inference, deduction and previous reading experience to find and appreciate meaning beyond the literal.' But, could I similarly justify this present discussion of felt tip pens, thin paper and glass panelled doors as pertinent to the children's literary development? Rather, as they struggle to make sense of implausibly all-knowing narrators, I become increasingly dissatisfied with the adequacy of the assessment requirements to reflect these children's competencies.

Genette (1980) states that 'Literature, like any other activity of the mind, is based on conventions, of which with some exceptions it is not aware.' (p.14) Yet it appeared that these six- and seven-year-olds *were* increasingly aware of conventions such as omniscient narrator, flashbacks in time and changes in points of view. Conventions that individual children spontaneously displayed in their oral narratives that we had been recording throughout the term were reflected more explicitly as we sat around on bean bags and talked about books. These two activities, oral storytelling and reflection, were beginning to offer a picture of the literary abilities of six- and seven-year-olds which ranged well beyond the expectations for this age determined by the devisers of Britain's National Curriculum.

It was to Genette that I had turned to provide a structure for my continuing analysis of their oral stories. Like Carol Fox before me, in her extensive analysis of 200 oral stories of pre-school children, I was anxious for an analytic system that would 'produce an account of *how* stories are told as well as *what* is told', and offer an analysis which overcame the tendency of story grammars 'to analyse plots, the events the narrative tells and to ignore the narrative as a communicative form' (Fox, 1992). In *Narrative Discourse: An Essay in Method* (1980) Genette makes explicit the distinction between the events the narrative recounts (the story), the telling of those events (the narrating) and the text itself (the narrative discourse) through his three major categories of **tense**, which is concerned with questions of chronology, **mood**, which deals with points of view and **voice**, which distinguishes between the narrating voice and the story the narrating voice is telling. As I analysed the children's oral stories using these categories, I found that whilst all existed in their simplest forms, more excitingly the children revealed an ability to manipulate these forms at a complex level.

Fox (1992) observes that 'the extensive variety of what children use their narrators to do indicates a high level of conscious control over the act of inventing and telling a story.' (p.14) Her literate pre-schoolers were experienced oral story tellers, but the evidence from children within my class who were mere novices with the tape-recorder, suggested that they too were developing an understanding of the difference between narrating and what is narrated. I was interested to discover if this was a selective literary competence or if they were all capable of such insights. It would have been a lengthy exercise to record and analyse a number of stories from each child in the class, so I decided that a discussion of a narrator's viewpoint in picture books during the library period would offer at least an impression of the children's 'conscious control' over the act of inventing and telling a story. Meek (1991) suggests that 'storytelling is a kind of game with rules'; just how aware were the children of these rules?

In the library I introduce the term 'narrator' to them by explaining who *in* the story is telling what is happening – but these six- and seven-year-olds who use words such as author, illustrator and publisher need no such simplistic explanations. '*Of course it's not the author, he's a real person,'* says Simon with ease. *'Yes, just like Anthony Browne at Waterstones,'* adds Charlotte with a familiarity borne of our afternoon with him. There are a few problems, for example why wasn't Bear telling his own story in *Bear Goes to Town? 'He needed Anthony Browne to tell it, because bears can only talk to other animals,'* suggests Joy. And if Bear was telling the story himself I enquire, how would he have told it? *'Well,'* says Jenny, *'He would have started off, "one day I went to town", not "One day* Bear *went to town." 'Yes, yes,'* adds Laura, *'If it says I did something then you know that person's telling the story.'*

When do you write something that says 'I went to town' I ask. *'In our diaries'* comes the reply. *'But they're not stories, they're real life,'* doubts Matthew. Jenny, perceptive as ever, counters, *'But they're really like stories for other people, they don't know it happened, we could have made it up.'* As indeed some children do, as testified by amused parents on Parents' Evening, who say, 'We never did that, our life is always the same at weekends.'

I set them to search out books that have the vital clue 'I' in them. Jenny corrects me, *'It could be we, if lots of people, a gang say, were telling the story.' 'But they might all tell different stories,'* says Matthew, *'Like when Aaron says Toby took something and Toby says he didn't.'*

There is some confusion. 'I' in speech marks particularly concerns them. 'I don't like the sound of that weather, Mrs G' says Mr Grinling in *The Lighthouse Keeper's Catastrophe. 'That's just Mr Grinling saying what he thinks,'* says Glen. *'Who knows what he thinks?'* asks Claire.

The mystery deepens. *'Well it must be someone who was there, just to know,'* adds Laura. *'You can't know what people are thinking'* contests Sam. *'You can if you write a book,'* says Sally. *'You have to know everything that's happening when you tell a story.'*

So who can it be? They look at the pictures for clues. *'It can't be Mrs G, she'd be cross with Mr G most of the time.'* Hamish the cat appears in much of the action. Hamish gets a vote. *'He must be telling the story, even if he doesn't say he is,'* suggests Toby. This last comment unleashes a string of metaphysical possibilities: *'Perhaps there was a boy there all the time, who isn't in the pictures but who knows everything that's happening,'* wonders Laura.

The unseen, unknown narrator is an appealing notion. The story world takes on a reality of its own made all the more exciting by invisible people, who are in on all the action but who never actually show themselves to the reader. The children search for them. Can it be another member of the gang in *Cops and Robbers? 'Yes, one without a name, he works for Grabber Dan.'* Elves accompany *Father Christmas,* elves who listen in and enjoy the 'Bloomin' swearing. Is it Mr Gumpy's wife? Is it the owner of the block of flats in *No Jumping on the Bed?*

They look for further clues, devouring picture books to discover who knows 'most' in the story, for this, by common agreement, must be the person who is able to tell that story. Thus, is it the miller in *Mouse Trouble?* Or is it the cat? Could it be one of the mice – yes, but which one, there's so many, they all look the same? Sometimes the oldest person is credited with telling the story, so it has to be George the babysitter in *Helpers,* although, after a brief flirtation with the idea that it is one of the sisters, there is common agreement that it must be the baby in *Peepo!*

Sometimes it is the most important name: *'Pooh tells all his stories.'* A doubter suggests Christopher Robin, as he is a boy and more able to tell what happens. *'No, he only knows what Pooh tells him, so it's got to be Pooh.'* The invisible appeals again: *'Perhaps when they think Christopher Robin's at home, he's always really watching what they do.'* But Pooh wins; his grandiose manner commands respect. *'Christopher Robin looks a bit like a girl,'* snarls Toby and all agreed, it must be Pooh. I don't follow up the obvious implication that girls can't tell stories.

Pictures give clues. In *Rosie's Walk* it *'Can't be Rosie, she doesn't know the fox is there,'* says Sophie. *'She knows,'* says Jenny, *'She just pretends she doesn't.'* But, *'It can't be the fox because he wouldn't have all those accidents.'* And there in the middle of the book is the evidence, an all-seeing goat. I enquire just where the goat can be in the pages where we don't see him. No problem, he's there watching – *'Behind the barn, the tree, the fence, the beehive.'*

They have no trouble taking on inanimate objects as narrators. It's the hat in Tome Ungerer's *The Hat. 'I think it might be the plum pie,'* hazards Matthew quietly after reading *Each Peach, Pear, Plum,* aware of the radical nature of his suggestion and fearful of laughter. It doesn't come for by now no one would suggest that plum pies can't tell stories.

'*There aren't many "I" books,*' moans Carley, after a twenty-minute search, '*we'll just have to write one.*' She's ready to abandon the library and return to the class writing corner. I suggest that she brings paper and pens into the library, 'like Class 6'. She is almost off when Glen finds *The Park in the Dark*. '*It's an "I" and a "we" book*':

> But there's not says Loopy, and I agree and Little Gee gets up
> on my back and we pass the Howl tree, me and Loopy and
> Little Gee. We're heroes, we three !

But which one's 'I' ? Little Gee is easy to identify on grounds of size, but who's Loopy ? There's a clue in the accompanying picture on the middle page – Little Gee is on the monkey's back – the monkey is 'I'. '*Monkeys are clever than elephants anyway,*' says Helen.

Just when they start to ponder this problem of intellectual superiority, up comes Natasha with *There's an Alligator Under My Bed*. '*This one's got an "I" in the title, a 'my' – my bed,*' she says excitedly. '*The narrator wrote the title too.*' The talk ranges on to titles. Just who does make them up is a point that we have never considered before, although we have talked at length about whether titles interest you straight away, or indeed make you reject a book without opening it. '*No,*' insists Mary Jane, '*authors make up the titles first, before they start the book, just like we write the title first before we write the story.*' I am chastised by this testament to my conservative writing processes; next week we'll make up the title last. Natasha listens, but she is adamant, '*The narrator wrote this title.*'

Our hour is up. Class 5 are waiting at the door. 'We'll take the book back to class and you can read it Natasha, line up at the door.' They tumble back past Class 5 straight onto the mat. By the time I've put our library record book back on the shelf, gathered up the stray jumpers and shoes, and returned to class, Natasha is sitting on our pink box, book in hand, her audience ready and waiting.

Ownership of *There's an Alligator Under My Bed* entirely her own, Natasha begins:

> There used to be an alligator under my bed.
> When it was time to go to sleep I had to be very careful,
> because I knew he was there.
> But whenever I looked, he hid... or something.

I encourage Natasha to share the pictures with the children. They are not deceived. 'Yes, yes' they chorus approvingly. 'He's there!' as jaws, tail and an eye are revealed beneath the green eiderdown. The narrator's parents are called but they fail to notice the alligator. The children warm to the apparent stupidity of parents.

> It was up to me. I just had to do something about that alligator.

The narrator of the story creeps from his bed and raids the refrigerator.

> I filled a bag with things alligators like to eat.

What alligators like to eat is just what Class 3 like to eat: peanut butter sandwiches, biscuits, fruit and sweets. A trail is laid through the house. It appears perfectly rational to the children that an alligator should be tempted by such goodies to leave his hiding place. He eats his way along the landing, down the stairs, through the hall and into the garage where:

> I slammed the door and locked it.

Victorious, the narrator returns to his bed. The children understand the narrator's satisfaction that:

> There wasn't even any mess to clear up.

But, there is a complication for the following morning with an alligator in the garage, father will have difficulty getting into his car. Natasha turns triumphantly to the last page.

> I'll just leave him a note.

And there in the picture are warnings written in a childish hand that Class 3 could have completed themselves:

> Dear Dad, there is an alligator in the garage if you need to wake me up. Be careful.

We discuss similar books we have in class with unbelieving parents in them: *Not Now Bernard*, and *There's a Hippopotamus on my Roof Eating Cake* are suggested. No problems here with who is telling the story.   Helen remarks, *'It's certainly not the Mum and Dad.' 'But what if ...' I suggest ... but they finish it for me, 'The alligator tells the story'.*   Out comes the paper roll, a piece is quickly torn off and fixed to the white board. We start with the title, and the children are keen to make suggestions: *There's a boy on top of my bed. 'No, the bed still belongs to the boy, not the alligator,'* points out Glen. *I'm under the boy's bed. 'Not very exciting, doesn't say anything about alligators,'* comments Toby. *I am an alligator and I live under a boy's bed.* No, that's too long. We settle for the rejected first suggestion and we start, me scribing at a furious rate to keep up with their ideas.

> I used to live under a boy's bed
> When it was time for him to go to bed he had to be very careful
> Because he knew I was there
> But wherever he looked, I hid... or something
> So he'd call his Mummy and Daddy
> But they never saw me
> It was up to him. He just had to do something about me
> So he went to the kitchen to get some bait to trap me
> He filled a bag full of things that I like to eat

We hit a problem. *'How did the alligator know what the boy was doing in the kitchen?' asks Laura. 'He followed the boy,' was the quick reply. 'That is not in the picture,'* she maintains. *'We'll have to change the picture too,'* suggests Sam.

> He put a peanut butter sandwich, some fruit and the last piece of apple pie in the garage
> He put biscuits down the hall
> He left fresh vegetables on the stairs

Same problem. *'It would change the whole story,'* complains Jenny *'if the alligator had to follow him around.' 'He could run back under the bed really quickly,'* suggests Thomas. *'Yes a magic alligator,'* adds Claire. *'No this a real story, not a magic story,'* corrects Helen.

> He put a drink and some sweets next to his bed. Then he waited and watched for me
> Sure enough, out I came to get something to eat
> The boy hid in the cupboard on the landing

He followed me down the stairs
He followed me into the hall
When I crawled into the garage
He slammed the door and locked it
Then he went to bed. There wasn't even any mess to clear up.

A further complaint. *'But how does the alligator know he's locked in the garage?'* *'He's got a key of his own.'* *'No, that spoils the end of the story. If he had a key he wouldn't stay there till morning, he'd get captured.'* *'The garage door's got glass in it.'* *'It hasn't in the picture.'* *'We'll change the picture. The door to my garage has got glass in it.'* The compromise was accepted by everyone.

Now that I'm in the garage, the boy wondered if his Dad
would have any trouble getting into his car tomorrow morning.

A real dilemma here. *'How does the alligator know what the boy is thinking?'* queries Claire. *'He knows everything,'* says Ross. *'Perhaps the boy said it out loud,'* suggests Laura. *'The alligator wouldn't be able to hear if he did say it, he's downstairs,'* Helen reminds us. *'The boy will have to say it on the other side of the door,'* says Sam *'we'll just change the picture again.'* *'But we'll have to put it before the bit about the boy going to bed,'* Jenny insists. *'If the alligator knows everything that's happening it wouldn't matter when it happens,'* continues Ross. This scenario is accepted; magic realism at seven years of age.

He just left his Dad a note.

The glass panel in the door theory is chosen again. *'The boy would have to use thin paper and felt tips so the alligator could read it through the glass,'* Simon suggests practically. *'Alligators can't read,'* states Laura, *'we said this was a real story.'* *'He doesn't need to read the note, he just knows they're notes to the boy's father,'* says Simon. *'If he can't read, how can he write the whole story?'* remarks Helen.

How indeed Class 3? But they're off again, and theories flow thick and fast. *'The alligator just told it to the author. The author wrote it down.'* *'He said it into a tape recorder.'* *'Perhaps he's a magic alligator who can write.'* *'Well, I think he must be anyway,'* says Laura, drawing our discussion to its close, *'because in real life alligators don't live under children's beds.'*

Not only did the children's responses reflect an understanding of Margaret Meek's 'rules' for storytelling, their enthusiasm and passion confirmed that, for them, storytelling was indeed a game. But how far did their queries and ideas unconsciously mirror Genette's categories? His category of tense appears relevant only to the extent that their re-telling of the alligator story represents a simple, chronologically correct narrative, told in the past tense, moving from event to event with little change in the pace. Rather, as the work focused on the narrator's viewpoint, the categories of voice and mood are more appropriate to the children's discussion.

A major concern for the children was how thought was represented in stories.

> 'I don't like the sound of that weather, Mrs G. *'That's just Mr Grinling saying what he thinks.'* (Referring to the sentence from *The Lighthouse Keeper's Catastrophe*.)
>
> *'How does the alligator know what the boy is thinking?'*
>
> *'You can't know what people are thinking.'*

Sally's response to the last point was, *'You can if you write a book, you have to know everything that's happening when you tell a story.'*

Their discussion reflects Culler's (1980) comment that in the real world,

> ... a speaker has certain kinds of information about events and lacks other kinds. He either experiences them or he did not, and generally he stands in a definable relationship to the events that he recounts. However true this model may be, there is nothing to prevent narratives from violating it and producing texts which involve impossible combinations. (p.12)

Whilst the children acknowledge that other people have thoughts and that cognitive processes have a role to play in story events (a major development from egocentric views), they still appear to demand that a narrator be close to events in order to have knowledge of them. This 'closeness' is variously explained as the character who knows 'most', the oldest person, or the most important character. All are a type of focalised narrative, where the narrator is inside the events of the story and shows the audience what is happening. But the children also recognise the potential for an omniscient, unseen, unnamed narrator, and find such invisible narrators particularly appealing. *'Perhaps there was a boy there all the time, who isn't in the pictures but who knows everything that's happening,'* they suggest, reflecting the idea of an unfocalised narration where the narrator stands outside the story and tells the audience what has happened.

When Jenny suggests that stories may be written in the first person plural, Matthew, based on classroom experience, mentions that more than one person might tell a different version of events. A discussion ensues in which the possibility is explored that Mr and Mrs Grinling would give conflicting reports of the action in *The Lighthouse Keeper's Catastrophe*. This beginning of an acceptance of a variable point of view is further evidence of the ability to decentre. The logic behind their ideas and questions is a model of how things operate in the real world. They reason that, *'The alligator wouldn't be able to hear, if the boy did say it, he's downstairs.'* They are not alone. Culler (1980) states 'It may well be that narratives will usually prove anomalous because our models of narrative procedures are always based on models of reality.' (p.12) However, the children are able to dismiss such anomalies by accepting that within stories all things are possible. *'If the alligator knows everything it wouldn't matter when it happens.'* They accept that the 'reality' of the text lies entirely within its narrative, and what confirms it as a story is its essential contrast to real life. For as Laura concludes, *'In real life alligators don't live under children's beds.'*

But then in the real world of formal assessment, six- and seven-year-olds are not expected to grapple with post-structuralist questions of narrator and narrative. They write stories, which are expected to be plausibly chronological, with a beginning, at least two characters, one event and an end. My children are showing how limited and inadequate a model of children's developing literacy competencies this is. Barthes (1970) observes that 'the goal of literary work is to make the reader no longer a consumer, but a producer of the text.' In discussions, these children showed striking powers of reasoning, argument, observation and below-surface reading as they moved towards becoming active producers of the texts they read.

In overcrowded primary classrooms where teacher time to read with individual children has been marginalised by equally overloaded curriculum demands, the opportunity to talk with groups of children must be exploited within language timetables. Such talk clearly gives insights into both children's developing awareness as readers and their cognitive capacities for logic, decentred thought, reasoning and imagination. We do not just need to read with, and to children, we need to stop and have conversations; conversations which may reveal to us more sophisticated literary competencies than we previously thought possible, particularly if the talk turns to alligators, glass-panelled doors, thin paper and felt tip pens.

References

Ahlberg, J. and A. (1978) *Cops and Robbers*. London: William Heinemann.

Ahlberg, J. and A. (1978) *Each Peach, Pear Plum*. London: The Bodley Head.

Ahlberg, J. and A. (1981) *Peepo!* London: Kestrel Books.

Armitage, R. and A. (1986) *The Lighthouse Keeper's Catastrophe*. London: Andre Deutsch.

Arnold, T. (1987) *No Jumping On The Bed*. London: The Bodley Head.

Barthes, R (1970) *SZ* (translated Richard Miller). New York: Hill and Wang.

Briggs, R. (1973) *Father Christmas*. London: Hamish Hamilton.

Browne, A, (1982) *Bear Goes To Town*. London: Hamish Hamilton.

Culler, J. (1980) Foreword to Genette's Narrative Discourse (see below).

Fox, Carol (1992) *Using Genette's Categories of Narrative Discourse to Analyse Young Children's Stories*. University of Brighton.

Genette, G. (1980) *Narrative Discourse: An Essay in Method*. (Translated Jane E. Lewin.) Ithaca: Cornell University Press.

Hughes, S. (1975) *Helpers*. London: The Bodley Head.

Hutchins, P. (1970) *Rosie's Walk*. London: The Bodley Head.

Meek, Margaret (1991) *On Being Literate*. London: The Bodley Head.

Meyer, M. (1987) *There's An Alligator Under My Bed*. London: J. M. Dent and Sons Limited.

Waddell, M. (1989) *The Park In The Dark*. London: Walker Books.

Ungerer, T. (1971) *The Hat*. London: The Bodley Head.

Yoeman, J. (1972) *Mouse Trouble*. London: Hamish Hamilton.

7

Debating punctuation: six year olds figure it out

Nigel Hall and Kate Holden-Sim

Background

For some years now, literacy researchers have placed children and their thinking at the centre of their investigations. This shift, led by a number of researchers (Clay, Goodman, Ferreiro and Teberosky and many others), has led a to renewal of interest in the way young children make sense of the literate world. Nowhere was this change more dramatic than in spelling development. After Charles Read's 1970 article was published the educational world viewed the learning and teaching of spelling in a different way. From viewing spelling as something that had to be learned from direct instruction, teachers began to understand how young children were busily constructing their own theories of how the spelling system worked, and that these theories were not stupid but carefully thought out and based upon evidence. Given the wealth of evidence, and not just from studies of spelling development, that children played a significant role in constructing their knowledge of spoken and written language, it seemed that no area of literacy had been left unresearched. However, somewhat by accident, some of us discovered a couple of years ago that studies into how young children came to understand notions to do with punctuation were remarkably scarce (see Hall, 1996a).

Punctuation is a major language component. It is centrally concerned with meaning and its neglect by the educational community seems strange. Its importance has never been underestimated by the world outside education as laments about the failures of people to punctuate correctly occur as regularly as complaints about spelling ability. Indeed its status in the new English National Curriculum came as a shock to many teachers of young children and the assessment of punctuation at age seven had such a depressing effect upon children's scores that the assessment authority removed it as a distinct component of assessment in 1995.

If children learn about literacy in the ways conceived by so many researchers, then is it the same where punctuation is concerned: do they go about constructing theories of how the punctuation system works and if so, how? In this report we offer some insight into how a few children began to help us see what was going on inside their heads. Such opportunities are not always available and many techniques used by researchers are manifestly poor at uncovering changes in conceptual understanding. Asking children questions about punctuation all too frequently results in the response 'I don't know'. However, it is clear to any teacher of young children that there is some serious thinking going on as young minds grapple towards achieving understanding of the complexities of the punctuation system.

The classroom

The children, at the beginning of this study, had been in school for one year and had just started the next academic year with a new teacher. The writing profiles for their first year at school showed no evidence of punctuation in any written work prior to this new year. During the Autumn term while there was no direct teaching of any punctuation concepts, the children were nevertheless introduced to punctuation in many different ways. In the first instance it was talked about. The children regularly had a story session using big books and the teacher frequently asked the children about what they could see on the page. After some of the children had pointed out punctuation marks, talk about them featured frequently in these sessions. The teacher offered minimal cues as to how they worked but she did use the names of the marks. The children worked frequently on the computer using the

Concept Keyboard; a full stop and a question mark were featured on this and not surprisingly were often used by the children, although not always correctly.

When the children undertook *Breakthrough to Literacy* work, the punctuation marks were in their folders and when a sentence had been constructed the teacher would usually ask them whether they needed anything else. Punctuation was frequently introduced by the children at this point. The teacher put a large sheet of paper out each day on which she left messages for the children. This created an opportunity to show her use of punctuation marks and the children frequently borrowed from her writing when adding their own comments on the sheet. Again, this message sheet provided a focus for discussion about punctuation as it did for many other aspects of written language.

Punctuation was a presence in this room but, although as a topic it came up frequently, it was not forced upon the children and they saw it then, and they still do, as something curious, interesting and to be explored. At no time did the children ever do exercises in punctuation and at no point were they corrected if, as was frequently the case, they got it wrong. As far as the teacher was concerned, punctuation was there to be explored by the children and she was interested in the ways in which they were making sense of the concepts. Her approach was to provide opportunities, experience, evidence and feedback rather than formal direct instruction.

The children

Three children were involved in the discussion reported below. Rachel was aged five years eleven months at the start of the study, Derek was five years eight months and Fatima was aged six years exactly. There is nothing in the work in their profiles to suggest that they ever used punctuation during their first year at school. When they first arrived in their new class, writing was done largely with *Breakthrough to Literacy* and carried out under the direction of the teacher. Soon afterwards, the richer experiences of writing and punctuation described above came into operation. All the children began to show interest in punctuation and from then on used it fairly frequently in their written work, although it was often unconventional. It also tended to be added after the writing had been completed (although this was not always the case).

All the children were in what has been described as the 'graphic phase' of punctuation (Hall, 1996b). In this phase, children tend to use sentence terminal punctuation not for linguistic reasons but to satisfy criteria associated with position on the page. Typical usage at this phase is putting full stops at the end of every line, putting a full stop only at the end of a page, putting one at the end of a story, or putting full stops through a piece because some are needed and must be scattered around. Although these can look like different uses of punctuation, Hall (1996b) argues that they are in effect one phase with slightly different surface manifestations depending upon the experiences of the child with teacher language or marking.

The situation

In this piece we are going to concentrate on the analysis of one event which involved the children in discussing punctuation and which suggests that some of them are beginning to explore the limitations of 'graphic' punctuation.

One of the major problems of studying young children's perspectives upon complex and abstract ideas is persuading them to be explicit about their beliefs. It is probably this difficulty which has resulted in the few existing studies into young children's punctuation relying solely upon analysis of texts. It is difficult to get young children to display thinking about linguistic issues. The technique devised in the event described below represents an attempt to put children in situations where differences in interpretation could become the subject of explicit discussion between the children, but where the incentive to explore the issues derives from the children not the researcher.

In this event a group of three children worked on orally constructing a text with one of the authors (KHS). Other groups also did this but in this chapter there is room to discuss only one group's discussion. KHS acted as a scribe only. Her brief was not to suggest anything but, if necessary, to keep the children on task. As one major problem of many children's books, and much children's writing, is that of one line sentences, she deliberately tried to avoid having what could be the ends of sentences at the ends of the lines she wrote on the paper. In a previous experience the group had constructed a story, while in the one discussed below they worked on a description of the class teacher. The story event took place in the classroom among all the other activities while this second event took place outside the classroom in a spare room. It was also video recorded, although the children were not aware of this as a miniature camera was used. In both cases the children knew that it was being sound recorded but as the researchers and the teacher had been sound recording work for two terms this was seen as quite normal by the children.

The children were invited to contribute the text. A number of possible procedural outcomes had been envisaged, for example, the children might simply jointly construct the text and at no time mention punctuation. If this had occurred the scriber would invite the children to look at the text after completion to see if there was anything they needed to add or examine. Only if this failed to elicit any comments about punctuation would the scriber have invited the children to consider whether any punctuation was needed. Alternatively, the children might make comments about punctuation during the scribing of the text. In this case the scriber would allow the discussion to continue until it was appropriate to move on.

The discussion

This event involved the children composing a mystery description of the class teacher and would be used later to see if anyone could guess who it was. This whole event lasted twenty-one minutes. There was a discussion about 'description' and the fact that other people were going to have to guess whose description it was. Rachel suggested 'She is my friend' and Kate wrote this on the easel. Derek instantly offered 'and sometimes she's a bit bossy'. On paper this looked as follows:

she is my friend and
Sometimes shes a bit bossy

Figure 1

Derek jumped up at this point, grabbed the pen and put a full stop at the end of the first and the second line. He then put two sets of marks, as shown in Figure 2:

she is my friend "and.
Sometimes she's a bit bossy.

Figure 2

KHS asked him what he had done:

Derek	Talk marks.
KHS	What are they?
Derek	Speech marks!
KHS	And why did you put them there?
Derek	Because we were speaking and the person wouldn't know that it was you who was speaking.

A number of the children had been noticing and using speech marks, indeed at one point it began to seem as if no one's work could be complete without a number of such marks. However, the appearance of speech marks on the printed page caused some confusion, as a much later part of the discussion made clear. When the children had completed dictating their text (see Figure 3) the issue of speech marks arose again.

At one point Rachel told Derek that he needed some more sets of speech marks but when he did so, Fatima challenged the form of the marks he had used:

Rachel	Two there and two there, silly!
Fatima	You've done it 'I I' (letter names), you used to say....
Derek	Yeah, but if it was 'I I' then they wouldn't be exclamation....
Fatima	When I did that you said 'Like this I I'

At this point Derek turned one set of speech marks into curved speech marks rather than leave them as straight lines.

Derek	Yeah, commas.
KHS	Are they still the same now they're commas?
Derek	Yeah.
KHS	How is it different?
Derek	'Cos they're nines and they're elevens. (*He points to his new 'speech marks'.*)

Speech marks were very important to Derek who sprinkled them liberally all over his writing and each time justified them as above, by saying they showed that it was him talking. The other children in this group had no trouble with that reasoning at all and concurred fully with it. This belief reveals a source of confusion for young children. Not unnaturally, teachers discuss speech marks by saying that they show when people are talking. But, of course, almost all children's writing is 'talked' when it is read aloud to the teacher or by the teacher. In this instance the text had been composed orally so, in a way, Derek is quite correct in asking for it to be recognised as speech written down. Derek is, in effect, representing the author's voice rather than a character's speech. Generally in this class, speech marks tended to be used randomly, but by the third term of the year several were using them with some degree of accuracy.

After the discussion about the full stops and speech marks in the first two lines, the composing and writing continued until the text was complete as below.

she is my friend "and.
Sometimes she's"a 'bit bossy.
and she shouts a lot and
she tells us to do our work
a lot sometimes just sometimes
she is very bossy shes got
long eyelashes

Figure 3

Once it was finished KHS slowly read the whole piece through but as the words were being read, both Derek and Rachel tried to grab the pen.

KHS	What do you want to put in Rachel?
Rachel	Comma.
KHS	Show me where?

KHS read the piece again, relatively slowly but using intonation as if there was sentence punctuation in the piece. Rachel put in two commas after 'bossy' on line 6. Derek wanted the pen but KHS said 'Maybe Rachel wants to put something else in'. Rachel said 'a full stop' and pointed to line 3 after the words 'a lot'. At this point an energetic and very complex debate followed between the three children. It is not an easy debate to follow partly because the children are trying to handle rather abstract ideas and partly because they make considerable use of anaphoric reference. We have tried to help the reader by offering some descriptions of actions and placements, and by referring to the turns in the conversation by numbers.

1	**Derek**	You're not supposed to put full stops in the middle.
2	**Rachel**	You are!
3	**Derek**	No, they're supposed to be at the end, Ooh!
4	**Rachel**	You are Derek.
5	**Fatima**	Yeah. So that's how you know that (*meaning the 'and' at the end of line 3*) goes with that (*meaning line 4*).
6	**Derek**	Yeah, but you see if you do one there (*meaning after 'lot'*), then it wouldn't be the end of the story... too long 'cos it wouldn't have 'and' on anymore.
7	**KHS**	Could you not say 'and' after the full stop?
8	**Rachel**	Yeah, but you can have full stops in the middle of ...
9	**Fatima**	Yeah, 'cos that (*meaning 'and' at the end of line 3*) goes with that (*meaning line 4*) Dante?
10	**Rachel**	Yeah.
11	**KHS**	(getting confused) So which bit goes with which Fatima? You show me. Let Fatima show us. So, where do you stop when you put the full stop?
12	**Fatima**	There (*points at 'and'*) 'Cos that goes with all that. (*Fatima shows where 'and' can be joined onto the next sentence on line 4 and Rachel agrees with her.*)
13	**Derek**	'Cos if it says all that (*meaning 'and she shouts a lot'*) and then it reads the other part (*meaning 'and she tells us to do our work'*) and then it says 'full stop' and then it says 'and', then it wouldn't make any sense.

93

14 **Rachel**	Yeah, but Derek that 'and' (*meaning the 'and' on the end of line 3*) belongs to that part of the words (*meaning line 4*).
15 **Fatima**	So they'll know.
16 **KHS**	Ah yes. Do you understand Derek?
17 **Derek**	I know what you mean, but if you did it there, say if you did it there (*points to end of line 3*) then it would look like a little man was kicking a football.
18 **KHS**	So, you are unhappy with that full stop in the middle Derek, aren't you? (*Derek gets a pen and crosses out 'and' with the intention of moving it to the beginning of line 4.*)
19 **Derek**	Well Rachel is quite right, because that's the end of that line (*he points to 'a lot'*) but then you start another word there (*indicates the newly written 'and'*) so it would be better if you started it there (*beginning of line 4*). (*Derek crosses out 'and' and writes it at the beginning of line 4 – see Figure 4*)

and she shouts a lot.
and
she tells us to do our work

Figure 4

This extract offers the clearest evidence suggesting that all these three children are in a state of transition from graphic to linguistic punctuation. When the first two lines had been written by KHS both Rachel and Derek agreed to having a full stop at the end of each line. While the full stop at the end of the first line is clearly incorrect, a slight error by KHS in writing the second line means that we do not know whether the second full stop was again a graphic placement or a linguistic placement. It is later, when Rachel wants to put the full stop after 'a lot' that the fun starts.

At first sight Derek appears quite firmly locked into placement based on the notion of line ending (turn 1 and 3) and he seems quite shocked at Rachel's transgression of those rules; the 'Ooh' in turn 3 stresses his dismay.   Equally, Rachel seems convinced that an alternative is permitted but is somewhat vague about it, offering a 'graphic' account ('in the middle' turn 8) rather than a linguistic account. It is when Fatima, who does not make many contributions to this discussion, offers her reason for Rachel's placement (turns 9 and 12) that the argument becomes a discussion rather than a contest of rebuttals. She locates the end-of-line 'and' as belonging to the unit on the next line, thus introducing a fluid notion of 'belonging together' based upon meaning rather than a fixed notion such as line ending.

Derek's response is difficult to interpret (turn 6). He seems to be struggling to find words to express his idea and this may be partly because he found himself under attack from both girls and having to justify his reasons at a deeper level His first statement seems to suggest that the full stop after 'a lot' is illegitimate because it leaves something lying around on the line – in his words 'it wouldn't be the end of the story'. Whether this is simply a restatement of the 'end of lineness' argument or whether he has the gleanings of something more powerful it is impossible to say.

As KHS tries to clarify what is being said, Rachel sticks to 'middle' while Fatima again explains the link between 'and' and the next line. Rachel agrees with Fatima but whether she is agreeing with the principle or the result is unclear.

Derek's next argument (turn 13) can be interpreted in a number of ways. Is he implicitly claiming some kind of linguistic rule that it is inappropriate to have a full stop before an 'and' as it artificially segments two linked pieces of text? We are inclined to think this is unlikely as there is no evidence in any of his written work that he recognises such a rule. It seems more likely that he is acknowledging the integrity of the two units under debate but cannot reconcile the way it works out visually as it confounds his other rule that full stops go at line endings. Thus the 'it wouldn't make any sense' in turn 13 seems to refer to the placement of the full stop rather than the 'sense' as the meaning of the two units.

In turn 14 Rachel now borrows Fatima's argument to try to convince him, but Derek appears to be feeling a bit overwhelmed by the opposition and in turn 17 seems to make a retreat away from the topic into a rather nice graphic description of the 't' of 'lot' and the full stop next to it. (We say 'appears' because later on Derek placed a full stop after 'lot' on line 5 of the description – see Figure 5.)

When he was challenged on this he justified it by saying that it was acceptable because his full stop was on the line (the imaginary base-line of the writing) whereas Rachel's full stop was above the line. Derek's ambivalence is resolved when he suddenly takes the pen, crosses out the 'and' at the end of line 3 and tells them that it would be better at the beginning of line 4. After that the discussion moves onto another point and the two girls seem to accept his repositioning. Either they recognise that there is some legitimacy in his action or they are simply fed up with arguing about it any more.

It seems that he has arrived at a solution which allows him to accept the legitimacy of Fatima's and Rachel's more linguistic position, but also allows him to maintain his belief in line ending as a criterion for full stop usage. It also seems to satisfy the two girls and it is likely that for all three of them the positions they are struggling with are rooted in the ambiguity of transition from dependence on graphicacy to acknowledgment of the integrity of some language units.

This analysis is necessarily a cautious one but to some extent its accuracy is not the crucial point of this chapter. It is the readiness of these children to explore through using oral language, the considerable complexities of a system like punctuation that is so significant. The group continue to discuss the punctuation of the text until it looks like Figure 5.

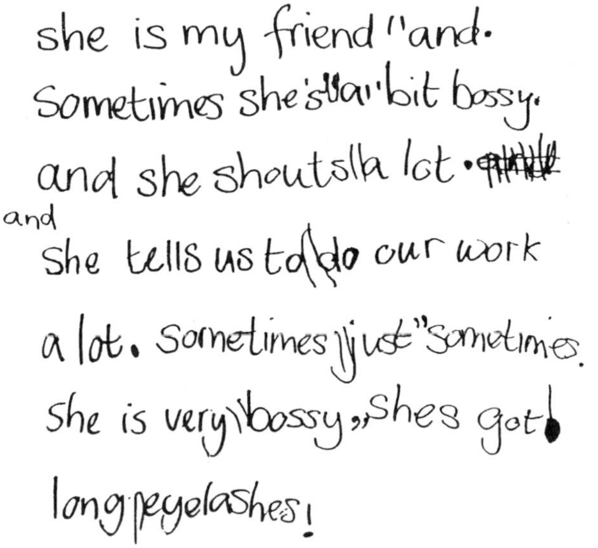

Figure 5

Later on the group is discussing the end of the description:

KHS	That's the end is it!
Rachel	Yeah. Put a full stop at the end. (*Rachel gets up, takes the pen and puts an exclamation mark at the end of line 7.*)
Rachel	I changed my mind.
KHS	Ooh, what have we got here?
Rachel	Exclamation mark.
KHS	Why have we got an exclamation mark at the end?
Rachel	'Cos she really means it.

A little later KHS said 'One thing we need to say is 'Who is it?' don't we, at the end.' Rachel wrote 'who is it' at the end of the sheet (see Figure 6). When Rachel had written the words KHS read the question with a question intonation. Derek shouted 'question mark'. Rachel then changed her exclamation mark into a question mark (Figure 6). Fatima noticed that when KHS finally reread it there was a pause between each of the three words (KHS had been reading it dramatically). Fatima put commas between each word (see below).

Figure 6

Conclusion

This chapter has been able to show only a small part of the discussion that took place. Virtually the whole of the discussion was about punctuation. There was no hesitation on the part of the children, nor any unwillingness to participate. The discussion was energetic, wide ranging and highly illuminating and would not have lasted as long as it did if the children had not wanted it to.

The discussion covered many aspects of punctuation including a rich range of punctuation marks. Commas, full stops, speech marks, question marks and exclamation marks were used, debated and amended. One child's theories confronted another's and the debates were hard-hitting as well as profound. What they show above all else is that the children were very actively involved in thinking about punctuation. It was not a take it or leave it phenomenon. It was not something they turned to with reluctance.

What is clear is that learning to punctuate is not a passive process. As has been made evident from studies in other areas of literacy development children are actively working out how the written language system works. Just as they create non-conventional versions of spelling patterns, so they generate non-conventional rules for punctuation. Although their rules may be non-conventional, the above extracts make clear that it is reasoning, not guessing that is involved. What is often not understood by adults is that it is virtually impossible to clarify children's reasoning with a few simple phrases. Almost anything that teachers can say about punctuation to young children is going to be partly right and partly wrong (see Arthur, 1996). Punctuation as a system is in a state of tension between its elocutionary origins and the later demands of grammarians and our choice of explanations often falls uncomfortably between the two. It should not be surprising that children experiment with our explanations but resolve them temporarily in ways which accord with their own experience of written language.

In many classrooms children do not get the opportunity to debate these notions, or if they do, teachers are not always around to hear them. It was our privilege to overhear these conceptual and linguistic explorations. We do not think these children were exceptional; indeed we believe the very opposite. They were not what many call privileged children: they did not come from well-to-do homes, and they attended an old school housed in a building that was not ideal. On the other hand they were privileged in being in a school which had staff who worked hard for all the children, and in being in a class where a teacher was sensitive enough to create interest in a topic and allow the children time and space to think it through.

The results reveal that a topic which has traditionally been seen as a merely routine and often boring skill, can actually be one which is interesting, even exciting to the children. More than that, it can be one which allows the children to disclose their enormous appetite for wrestling with the complex conceptual problems that arise in understanding written language.

References

Arthur, C. (1996) 'Learning about punctuation: a look at one lesson.' in Hall, N. and Robinson, A. (eds) *Learning About Punctuation*. Clevedon: Multilingual Matters.

Hall, N. (1996a) 'Learning about punctuation: an introduction and overview' in Hall, N. and Robinson, A. (eds) *Learning About Punctuation*. Clevedon: Multilingual Matters.

Hall, N. (1996b) Final report for ESRC Project, Learning to punctuate: an ecological and conceptual investigation. ESRC Research Grant R000221380. (In preparation).

Read, C. (1970) 'Pre-school children's knowledge of English phonology.' *Harvard Educational Review*, 41, 1, 1–34.

The work reported here is part of the project 'Learning to punctuate: an ecological and conceptual investigation' and is funded by the Economic and Social Research Council.

8

Children talking about the past

Pat Hoodless

Background

Most teachers would probably agree that children below the age of seven or eight find 'the past' and 'time' difficult concepts. These notions are essentially abstract and children's ability to talk about them often appears very limited. Young children often make inaccurate attempts to estimate time or to recall when something happened and this has convinced many teachers, and academics, that history, with its reliance on having some understanding of both time and the past, is an inappropriate topic in early years education.

Research into children's understanding of time and the past prior to the 1970s was generally very pessimistic. Oakden and Sturt (1922) found that before the age of nine, children's concepts of the past were 'shallow and nebulous'. Children were unable to cope with anything beyond the span of one or two generations and had very little grasp of dates. Subsequent work, often taking Oakden and Sturt as the starting point, tended to arrive at similar conclusions, finding that children below the age of ten could not deal with temporal relationships. Piaget (1967) concluded that children found time and the past difficult concepts, his findings suggesting that six-year-olds could not arrange pictures in a sequence, understand the length of durations, measure time using a standard scale, or understand simultaneity.

The work of Jahoda (1963), a social psychologist, tended to emphasise children's lack of understanding of the past. He found that before the age of five, children were unable to describe a recent event or sequence pictures and that soon after the age of five were capable of ordering events only into 'earlier and later' and that success was contingent upon the children's familiarity with the content of the task. His work suggested that by the age of five or six children could understand 'yesterday, today and tomorrow', by age seven or eight they could grasp fully the concept of 'week', by the age of nine or ten the concept of 'months', by age ten or eleven 'seasons' and it was not until early adolescence that they could fully understand 'last year, this year or next year'.

Such studies tended to confirm the belief that dealing in historical concepts with young children was difficult or indeed, even inappropriate. Were these commonly held views of young children's learning rather inadequate responses to what children say about time and the past? Many of the errors young children make are associated simply with the measurement of time. However, a failure to understand the accurate quantification of time is not the same thing as failing to have any concept of time. Too much identification of children's failures with historical time may have interfered with being able to acknowledge what they can, and do, understand about time and the past. In more recent years research has tended to focus less on what children cannot do and more upon the ways in which they move towards an understanding of the past. In this chapter I want to explore the ways in which some young children are beginning to make sense of the past.

Language is the principal medium through which ideas about time and the past can be explored. Therefore, I decided to create a number of different learning experiences related to time and the past, during which I could observe and record children's talk. The events were generally carried out in fairly informal, small group situations. The main focus was to discuss a story that had been shared with the children and which raised particular issues to do with time and the past. I also introduced activities such as the solving of an historical problem through investigating 'clues' in the form of objects, pictures, or stories.

The intent of these sessions was to offer children the opportunity to talk about things which had notions of time and the past embedded in them. I wanted to understand how children talked about time and the past. I was not looking for their errors but was listening to how they were beginning to make sense of complex concepts. In this chapter I am first going to consider how the children made sense of the passing of time both in relation to relatively recent past and the distant past. Later on I will consider how they begin to understand what it means to be 'in the past.'

Time passing

From random conversations and observations, it is evident that some children acquire understandings about the past at quite an early age. My own three-year-old frequently referred to 'fashioned-old' cars – this being a passion at the time. He would make this reference to toys or real cars seen out in the street, always correctly. Another four-year-old child would frequently refer to 'the new days', suggesting a broader awareness that things can be divided up into 'old' and 'new'. I had also noticed that when young children talked about the books they were reading or having read to them, elements to do with time were frequently mentioned. Consequently many of the discussions reported in this chapter arose from talk about children's fiction books.

Apart from the fact that the passing of time is a critical feature of narrative, many authors of children's books play with the notion of time in their books. John Burningham's *Come Away From The Water, Shirley,* and Maurice Sendak's *Where The Wild Things Are* are wonderful examples of this. Both books play with the phenomenology of time passing. In both books the child's version of the story is at odds with that of the adults in the book. In *Come Away From The Water, Shirley* each double-page spread contains on one side the simply and sparsely coloured rendition of Shirley's parents sitting on the beach, and on the other the amazing technicolour adventures that Shirley is having – adventures that involve being captured by pirates, walking the plank and so on. The mundaness of the parents' world is contrasted with the intensity of the child's world. In Sendak's book the child also goes off experiencing stunning adventures and yet returns home to find his dinner still hot on the table.

When I talked to the children in this study, words to do with the measurement of time occurred throughout the conversations, although they were not always used accurately. Clock time was referred to spontaneously by three- and four-year-old nursery children when discussing *Come Away From The Water, Shirley:*

PH	Is it daytime or night time? (*Pointing to a daytime picture*)
Child	Daytime.
PH	And this one? (*Pointing to a picture shown in darkness*)
Child	Eleven o'clock. Night time because it's black. It's too dark, but when it's morning, it can be eleven o'clock in the morning.

The confusions generated by having a twelve hour clock system have been conquered by this child, who is pleased to display his knowledge of time measurement. There were many attempts to refer to the passing of time or to indicate the past by mentioning days or years. After studying the illustrations in the same story, a group of seven-year-olds made the following estimations about the length of time Shirley spent on the beach.

Child	Oh, about a day.
Child	A day and half a night.
Child	Just a day.
Child	Just when the sun's setting.
Child	There was dark all around her.
Child	Yes, look, you can see the moon, and the sun's there as well.
Child	The sun's setting in the sky, that's what you can see sometimes, the sun and the moon in the sky both together.

[A discussion about their observations follows.]

Child	I think Shirley's been on the beach for a day and half a night.
Child	I think the night time is just a dream.

By using the illustrations carefully, they were teaching each other about careful observation, estimation and the importance of sharing and pooling ideas based on these observations and on

103

their personal experiences of seeing the sun and moon in the sky. Through this kind of discussion they were using and testing their knowledge about time and linking it with calculation, building up between them as accurate an estimation as was possible from the information available to them.

Precise measurement of time in hours and minutes featured more frequently in the talk of seven-year-olds. In a similar discussion about how long the adventure had lasted in *Where the Wild Things Are*, one child tried to be very precise about his timing:

PH	Was it a long time?
Child	An hour and ten minutes because when me and my grandma went for a walk in the woods it took us half an hour there and ten minutes to get there as well as an hour.
PH	Is ten minutes longer than an hour or shorter?
Child	(*All*) Shorter.

This child is not only justifying his estimation, he is revealing much about how he has internalised his understanding of time measurement. Clearly, he has learned about durations and linked these with precise clock timings by relating his own experiences to the conventional system for measuring time.

Some children, by the age of seven, can make quite accurate estimations of time. The following responses were given to questions about the relative lengths of time spent on the beach by Shirley and her parents in *Come Away From The Water, Shirley:*

PH	How long do you think they were actually there, on the beach?
Child	About two or three hours.
Child	About two and a half hours.
Child	Three hours.
PH	How long did her dream seem to last?
Child	In the story it seemed to last like a long time really.
Child	Yes.
Child	Because it lasted over day, night, day, day, day...

These seven year-olds were in no doubt that while her parents sat on the beach for only a few hours, Shirley, in her fantasy play, was away for days and nights. They exhibited understanding of the significance of these terms as time markers and were able to use them appropriately.

A group of six-year-olds seemed to have no problem with the notion of the experience of time being relative:

PH	How long do you think Shirley's adventures seemed to go on for?
Child	Quite a long time.
Child	About a day because it was morning, and it shows you at night there – it's all dark, there it's not...
PH	So what seemed to happen to the time for Shirley?
Child	It went longer.
Child	It seems longer when you're imagining things.
Child	Yes, like when you fall asleep, you think it's just a short time, but it's not.
Child	And like in assembly, it feels a long time.

They appear to have quite a complex understanding of how durations of time can appear to vary, depending upon how they are experienced, despite the fact that children of the same age characteristically have difficulty with conventional clock time. No doubt their understanding of this notion is aided and abetted by many things at school other than school assemblies.

A group of seven-year-olds, talking about *Where The Wild Things Are* revealed conceptual understandings of different aspects of time. The children had just concluded that Max had been dreaming about the Wild Things:

PH	Why do you think his supper was still hot? How did it get into his room?
Child	A dream.
Child	Because it was only a dream and he hadn't gone for a year away.
Child	I think he was asleep, because he's itching his eyes. His Mum put it in while he was having his dream and didn't want to wake him up.

PH	What's happening in this part, when he has all these adventures with the Wild Things?
Child	I don't think it's true...
Child	He's dreaming. I don't think that forest can stay there for a long time and talk to people (?)
Child	Because he was dreaming, it's because he thought of it before he went to sleep and he's dreaming it all out.

Here the children are aware that time can pass at a different rate when dreaming (see also Chapter 5). They are also aware of the concept of simultaneity, pointing out that Max was asleep when his mother put his supper in his room. There is awareness of what is true and untrue; reality and unreality and some understanding of devices used in stories. The children are using the real sequence of inferred events in order to rationalise what happened. Sequencing skill, inferential ability, in the sense of inferring what happened 'behind the scenes', concepts of cause and effect and a grasp of some of the subtleties of time are all apparent in talk such as this.

Chronological measurement over long periods of time is generally considered one of the most difficult aspects of the past. After listening to the story of the Three Bears, I asked a different group of children in an inner city school whether they thought that events of this kind could happen today:

Child	A long time ago...
PH	In 1994?
Child	If it was true it would start about sixty years ago.
Child	About five thousand years ago.

In this case, the children's estimations are random. Their guesses do provide, however, some indication of what children of this age mean by the phrase 'a long time ago'. Both sixty years and five thousand years are 'a long time'. Responses which appear wild or inaccurate, on the surface, are often, on further reflection, little different from what an adult might say, except that, in this case, an adult might have in mind a particular historical period in which such an incident might occur.

One seven-year-old was able to place events chronologically with surprising accuracy. After some discussion of, and a story about, the discovery of America, I asked his group:

PH	How long ago do you think this all happened?
Child	Nine centuries.
Child	Six centuries.
Child	Seven centuries.
Child A	Five centuries.
PH	And how many years would that be?
Child A	Five hundred years.
Child	It was four years that it took then? (*for Columbus to reach America*)
Child	Four weeks.
Child	Two weeks.

Child A clearly understood the meaning of the word 'century' as well as giving the correct number of centuries in this case, while the other children were using the strategy of making random guesses to test out on the teacher which guess was the most accurate. In addition, these children were clear in their minds that while all this happened centuries ago, the actual journey only took years, or, as the children corrected themselves, weeks. (Columbus was actually at sea only a matter of weeks, so the children's conclusions were fairly accurate.)

The same group, later talking about a book in their classroom which was well known to them, made the following comments:

PH	How long ago do you think the dinosaurs were on the earth?
Child	A million years.
Child	A million and one hundred years.
Child	And when you go where the dinosaurs lived you can see a bone.
PH	So, would the dinosaurs have been around before Christopher Columbus or after?
Child	(*several*) Before!
PH	A long time before?
Child	(*all*) Yeah.
Child	Five centuries before it.

The beginnings of chronological understanding are evident here.

The children know that, in talking about dinosaurs, they must use terms such as 'millions' and know that this would all have occurred before the time of Columbus.

Children between the ages of three and seven evidently try to use the terminology of time measurement, albeit imprecisely at first. What is surprising is the degree of accuracy achieved by certain children at a very early age. Having observed these particular children listening and working at other tasks in their classes, it was apparent that these were the very observant children, who paid close attention in lessons, took in and memorised details. While it is impossible to suggest reasons for their ability, I would infer from their exceptional performances that they had benefited from the attention focused upon history in their classes and possibly from additional support at home.

Understanding the past

Some of this work carried out with young children gives us information about how they begin to make sense of and understand the past. Looking at the strategies which these children used in explaining their understandings about past periods in time, enables us to see how this knowledge develops and how children are eventually able to distinguish between particular historical periods. At first, children may show an awareness of broad chronological distinctions, as these four-year-olds do when talking about Shirley's adventure on the pirate ship:

PH	When did this happen, now or a long time ago?
Child	A long time ago because of the boats, sail boats.
Child	If it was now, there wouldn't be monsters now, monsters like dinosaurs.
Child	Pirate boats.
Child	There's no such thing as pirates. Well, there could of, millions and zillions years ago.
PH	Could it happen today?
Child	No.
Child	It was about sixty years ago.
Child	Treasure could be true, because there's gold under the ground. It could be true five days ago.

The broad distinctions that these children draw are to do with what belongs or doesn't belong in a certain period of the past and with the notion of sequences, of what comes before or after a given event. They were aware that boats with sails belonged to a time before the present. They knew that dinosaurs belonged to a much earlier time, perhaps before the sailing boats. They also knew that treasure can be found now, as well as in the time of the pirates, since it's under the ground and could still be there. Not only are they revealing their knowledge here, but also a grasp of the key historical concepts of change and continuity. They know what has gone for good. They also know that other things still exist. The following discussion and transcripts show that these central concepts about the past are refined as children acquire broader general knowledge and information about periods in history. Some specific strategies that the children use as they develop their understanding about the past are examined more closely in the next section, beginning with sequencing, an organising method evident in the transcript above.

Sequencing strategies

Activities which involve children in sequencing require them to organise events or objects according to time. Sometimes this is in general terms, such as, what happens first, next or last and sometimes in more specific terms, such as identifying dates or the events which occurred in the same historical period. Observing children when they are engaged in sequencing tasks affords opportunities for evaluating the strategies they use and the concepts they hold.

Most children aged four or five are able to retell a story which they have just heard, with help or prompting from illustrations in the book. This ability to recall a narrative is an early form of sequencing, perhaps, where the logical series of events is recognised and committed to memory. Another kind of sequencing ability involves the children in reorganising information into a sequence which they have created according to their own criteria. I spent some time with a class of four- and five-year-olds, talking about sequences and comparing these with the number lines they had on their classroom wall. I then asked them to put in order a set of four stereotyped historical pictures from different periods in the past. The people depicted were from the Neolithic, late medieval, English civil war and modern space ages.

Most of the children clearly did not understand the purpose of the task, pushing the pictures around on their desks at random. One child, however, quickly ordered the pictures correctly, from left to right across his table. I assumed this must have been pure coincidence and went to talk to him about his pictures. He described picture one as coming first, because it was a picture of a cave man. He knew that the space traveller could be 'now'. When asked about the middle two pictures, by far the most difficult to place, he still replied quite confidently, that the people in picture two went next because 'they had more fancy clothes', and the third picture went in that position because 'they had buildings with big windows like that'. Each statement was accurate, the pictures correctly sequenced and logical explanations given, indicating a considerable knowledge and understanding about different times in the past. This child, like those mentioned earlier, was clearly able to make exceptional observations and statements, possibly due to rich early experiences and to talk about the past with adults. Indeed, he did say that he had looked at pictures like this at home. The reactions of the other four- and five-year-olds suggest that this task lies outside of their experience and understanding of earlier periods in time.

Considerable skill in ordering pictures from different times in the past was observed in another class of four- and five-year-olds in an inner city multicultural school, where a great deal of time had previously been spent on sequencing activities. I presented the children with a collection of cars from different times in the past and asked them to put them in order, oldest to newest. Working in small groups on the task, all the children were able to sequence the pictures. Some placed them in reverse order, but still produced the correct sequence in terms of time order. One difficulty in monitoring talk during this kind of task was that very little actually took place. The children tended to work individually at sorting their pictures, concentrating more upon manipulating the cards than on talking about them. I found I was having to talk to the children in a somewhat artificial way, generally resulting in teacher-led series of question and answer sequences.

However, the children were able to explain that some cars were older, so they went first, then they got newer and newer. They could distinguish between old and new and between older

and newer, in different historical periods. In this case, the strategy
used was to employ these general terms to justify allocating the
cars to different periods in time. A comparison was being drawn
between what is old and what is new or newer, so the judgements
were based on comparison in a very rudimentary way. A similar
strategy was used by the child in the previous example when he
associated the space traveller with 'now' and not with the past,
which could be seen as 'then', both being very broad distinctions
in time. The same child used a further strategy when he identified
what belonged to specific eras by noting that 'they had' particular
clothes or buildings. Already, some four- and five-year-olds can be
seen to have strategies for understanding the past.

Noticing differences and similarities

Another piece of conversation suggested processes by which
children learned how to distinguish between past and present.
During a quiet drawing session with a class of seven-year-olds, I
brought over a book which the children had heard many times
and which was a great favourite with them. The book was *Peepo!*
by Allan and Janet Ahlberg which is set in Britain during the
Second World War. The illustrations are of domestic scenes and are
rich with details which include an old-fashioned bath, fireplace,
sink, and items specific to that time, such as a gas mask. I began
to talk about it casually, noting the children's responses:

PH	Do you think that story is about nowadays?
Children	(*all*) No!
Child	Because it hasn't got any telly.
Child	And the teapot...
Child	And they don't have erm, electric...
Child	And they got...
Child	They have got electric.
Child	They don't have a bath like that.
Child	I know they have electric light...
Child	I've found something else.
Child	Coal.
Child	That picture...
PH	There's a strange thing on the shelf here. Whatever is that?

Child	Oh, a mask.
Child	That's a gas mask.
PH	When did they need a gas mask, I wonder?
Child	Oh, yes, when there was... like... when Germany comes...like...and they...
Child	When there's armies.
Child	Fifty years ago, in the Second World War.
Child	I watched a film about a man who was in the future and they got down on the floor.
Child	Oh, yeah. I watched that film.
Child	Was it *Dr. Who* or *Back to the Future*?
Child	And there's something else. Let's turn back and look at it.
PH	Oh, yes. It's an old-fashioned radio.
Child	Look at that. They used to hang their clothes on there, 'cause they didn't have a washing line then, so they make it, so they put it over the wire.
Child	And they don't have... like us. And we got bigger ones.
Child	And these socks look different.
Child	Miss, I've remembered something else. I remembered something else ages ago. That clock.
Child	It ain't a clock it's a radio.
Child	Oh, yeah – it's like a clock.
Child	And that girl!

Their teacher had previously read this story to the class in connection with the recent VE day celebrations and had spent some time encouraging them to observe the detail in it. Producing the book caused great excitement and generated spontaneous comment, discussion and personal reflections. There was considerable use of appropriate terminology and some accurate reference to the historical time shown in the illustrations.

In comparing detail in the pictures with 'what we have now', the children were employing the concept of similarity and difference, moving beyond the notion of what 'they had' to include what 'they didn't have'. The children also used the strategy of relating new learning or observations to personal experiences, such as the watching of the film *Back to the Future*. At age seven, these children obviously have more experience and knowledge about the world than the four- and five-year-olds had in the previous examples. They can apply this when trying to understand the past and, from the rapid pace at which the children worked, making and discussing numerous observations, they enjoyed doing it as well.

Location and the process of historical enquiry

During discussion with a group of seven-year-olds, arising from a problem-solving task on the Romans, it is possible to see how children begin to understand the process of historical enquiry:

PH	So what do you think all these clues have told us then?
Child	That he collected coins must mean he's an archaeologist. He wouldn't have been alive in Roman times, would he? He would be alive something like now and he probably found them in his garden or somewhere.
PH	Yes, so what does it tell us about his house and where he lived?
Child	A Roman building?
Child	... something Roman there...
PH	Yes, where would the Roman things have been?
Child	The Romans must have been there.
Child	So he was ... so his house was on top of a Roman ruin.
Child	Mrs. Hoodless, did the Romans live there before he sort of like, so they were ... and they left these coins there?
PH	They might have done. Yes. Our school is on the site of a Roman camp. There was a Roman camp here 2000 years ago.

In this small extract we can observe children engaging with the notion that the same place may have been inhabited by people throughout successive historical periods. They touch on the idea that objects left behind in the past might be found in the present and give clues to the way the earlier inhabitants lived. Investigating a location and its artefacts in this way is a central strategy in the process of historical enquiry and one in which these children are beginning to show both interest and ability.

Imagining and speculating about the past

Another strategy which children use in talking about and understanding the past is that of speculating about people and events and imagining what might have happened. Below, another group of seven-year-olds are talking in groups about a problem-solving task, using story, artefacts and documents.   The task involved the children in investigating a box of objects to piece together a story about an old man who had recently died. The box contained items relating to Roman times, suggesting the man had antiquarian interests. However, his own spectacles were also found in the box, creating a dilemma for the young investigators.

PH	What about the other things that were found? What about the broken glasses?
Sharon	It could have been the old man's and when he died, something could have happened to them to get broke ... something could have fallen on them.
PH	Yes. Do you agree with that, do you think they are likely to have belonged to the old man – the broken glasses?
Claire	Well the Romans could could have knocked his glasses off and cracked them.
Children	(*Several*) No.
Josh	The old man wouldn't be alive. The old man wasn't alive when the Romans were here.
Kath	He would have been 2000 years old.

The nature of the task in this example has encouraged the children to speculate about what 'could have' happened and they can be seen using this term several times. Through this strategy they can begin to examine the possibilities and to notice, as they most decidedly do, when anachronistic suggestions are made. In order to notice which suggestions fit and which don't they have to draw upon their existing knowledge of the historical period under discussion. However, the opportunity to use this knowledge and to explore it is provided by the initial speculating and imagining. In particular, Claire's anachronistic remark about the Romans and the glasses resulted in some children giving reasons why the two events could not have occurred in the same historical time, by pointing out the lack of simultaneity between the times of the

Romans and that of the old man. The speculation also allows Kath, in the final comment, to reveal her accurate and detailed chronological understanding about the past.

The use of small group work in this example, and many/most of the previous ones, is worth mentioning. There can be little doubt that the kind of interaction which occurs in small group discussion enhances children's social and intellectual skills. They learn to collaborate with others, sharing ideas and accepting other points of view. From discussion with peers and adults they learn the use of terminology appropriate to time and the past, broadening its scope and testing its accuracy on others. Most importantly, perhaps, they learn how to think and learn for themselves. They frequently make connections between first-hand experiences and new information about the past, thus placing an aspect of the past within an understandable conceptual framework for themselves. In relating their own experiences with those of others, they are also embarking upon the difficult process of empathising, identifying with the experiences of others, an essential skill in history. Discussion enables them to engage in the process of ordering, sequencing and rationalising events, so that they become better able to quantify time and imagine both the distant past, as in the examples here, and the future.

Implications for teachers and teaching

There is a clear need for teachers to plan opportunities and facilities for children to engage in talk about the past. The pace and range of learning through peer group discussion is such that it merits serious consideration as a teaching strategy. The value of such talk is self-evident in a number of ways. It motivates and stimulates children allowing them to explore their conceptual understandings at a familiar, accessible level of discourse and using the strategies that best suit their level of experience and knowledge. It enables the teacher to reduce the level of demand upon him/herself, providing time and the opportunity to listen to and assess the children's understanding.

In assessing learning in this way, talk reveals to the teacher the true extent of children's awareness of the past, since they are not inhibited by other factors, such as talk couched in adult terms, or reading material at a difficult level. A problem which I experienced myself, and one which I observed in other teachers, was the pressing need to provide constant input for the children. I was aware that I was talking too much, dominating the conversation, or at worst, interrupting the children's line of thought. The major implication here is the need for teachers to listen to children talking rather than constantly talking to them. Teachers are then more likely to become aware of the wide divergence in understanding about the past in young children and of the complexity of understanding which some children possess at a surprisingly early age.

References

Ahlberg, J. and A. (1981) *Peepo!* London: Kestrel Books.

Burningham, J. (1977) *Come Away From The Water, Shirley.* London: Jonathan Cape.

Jahoda, G. (1963) 'Children's concepts of time and history', *Educational Review,* 15, 87–104.

Oakden, E. C. and Sturt, M. (1922) 'The development of the knowledge of time in children', *British Journal of Psychology,* Vol.12, 309–336.

Piaget, J. (1967 orig. pub. 1927) *The child's conception of time.* London: Routledge and Kegan Paul.

Sendak, M. (1963) *Where The Wild Things Are.* London: The Bodley Head.

9

Assessing a bilingual child's talk in different classroom contexts

Charmian Kenner, Kay Wells and Helen Williams

Even before the rise of interest in oracy in classrooms, the quality and quantity of bilingual children's talk was being monitored in some way by many teachers. Whereas it could be assumed that most children with English as a first language would 'naturally' develop oral skills so long as a rich learning environment was provided, second language learners were often viewed differently. In these cases, it was often the teacher's impression of the ability to use spoken English which became the basis for evaluating progress and educational potential in all areas of the curriculum.

There is evidence to suggest that teachers may, often unconsciously, have low expectations of bilingual children (Emblen, 1990; Levine, 1990) and that this can affect their perceptions of the child's contribution in class. Firstly, the teacher may create fewer opportunities to hear bilingual children talk. In a study by Biggs and Edwards (1994), teachers who intended to treat all children 'the same' actually interacted more frequently with white children, and had significantly fewer extended exchanges with ethnic minority children. Secondly, a teacher may expect certain types of talk from children in particular classroom situations, without realising that these 'normal' spoken exchanges are in fact culturally specific. For example, Gregory (1994) has shown how Tajul, a bilingual five-year-old, had to learn to talk with his teacher in an accepted style when reading a storybook together.

In Britain, teachers are increasingly being asked to assess bilingual children's talk with respect to fluency, vocabulary range, and grammatical accuracy, in order to categorise children's needs for support purposes. This chapter raises questions about how such assessment can be carried out in a way that most accurately represents a child's abilities. It also asks who is to make the judgments: will language support-teachers, class teachers, assistants and helpers have access to different information about talk, according to the contexts and relationships in which they work with children? Finally, what factors do we need to take into account when developing our understanding of bilingual children's knowledge of structures and vocabulary?

The case study which may help to illuminate these questions arose, unplanned, in an inner-city nursery class in South London. Kay Wells is the school's language support teacher whose task is to aid the development of bilingual children's language within the mainstream curriculum. Kay had been asked to assess the spoken English of several children with whom she had little previous contact. Although such a one-off situation may be comparatively rare, it did serve to bring into focus some of the difficulties which lie at the heart of language assessment. The main evaluation activity of looking at a book together produced surprisingly little response from Meera, a four-year-old whose first language is Gujarati, and who is considered by her class teacher, Helen Williams, to be quite talkative in English.

Helen, whilst being convinced from everyday classroom experience that Meera could produce a rich range of spoken language, had no specific examples to hand; such evidence is hard to collect, whilst written language is, of course, easily demonstrated. She therefore decided to try to note down phrases used by Meera in future interactions. Meanwhile, she mentioned the discrepancy in assessments to Charmian Kenner, a researcher who was working in the nursery looking at early writing in English and in children's home languages. Audio-recordings made for Charmian's research included Meera's participation in socio-dramatic play, and her conversation with Charmian and with other children in the nursery's writing area.

The three of us met to comment on extracts from these notes and transcripts, and to explore ways of evaluating Meera's talk. This half-hour meeting was also taped. Our discussion produced a number of ideas which would not have occurred to us singly. These were regarding Meera's spoken language and regarding the potential of different assessment contexts. These insights are shared here in the hope that they could be relevant to the evaluation of other bilingual children in classroom situations.

The evidence

First, we looked again at Kay's notes from her assessment interview with Meera. Kay had chosen to use a colourful picture book by Richard Scarry, showing everyday scenes and activities. She knew that this was usually popular with young children and hoped that it would be conducive to conversation. However, Kay's comments, reproduced below, reveal that the exercise was less productive than she had hoped.

> *Notes made for nursery records – January 1995*
>
> *Meera:* for a van, bus and train, she just repeated 'bus'.
> On page about the home, she said 'eating' for mum
> cooking with a pan, and in the bedroom, just
> volunteered 'mirror'. Birds bathing in bird bath,
> 'eating'. Correctly said the sofa was blue. Unsure
> about the playground and relevant vocabulary. I was
> surprised at the limited nature of the language used.

Meera's monosyllabic responses in this situation contrasted sharply with the first transcript we examined; this shows her participating in 'pretend play' with a non-bilingual friend, Ebony, in the nursery's role play area. We focused on the following extracts:

> *Children talking in the home corner – October 1994*
>
> **Ebony**   Meera's my sister, I'm the mum, and Stefanie's the
>   doctor.
> **Meera**   I am dad!
> **Charmian**   You're dad are you, OK.
> **Meera**   And you are – you're the mum. You the auntie!

119

Charmian	All right, I'm the auntie then.
Meera	No – you kid!
Charmian	All right, shall I be your sister?

(Later)

Ebony	If I say, 'wiggle your hands up the air', that means you got to drink now. (*Referring to the nursery routine of coming to the teacher, with your hands in the air, to show you are ready for drinks time.*)
Charmian	Oh – where are we then?
Ebony	In your school! Everybody put your hands up, up the air.
Charmian	Oh! (*Does so.*)
Ebony	We're going to have assembly and PE, and we are going to do a register first, everybody put their hands down.
Meera	And if you listen – if you don't listen, you are sitting somewhere else, you are sitting on a chair near a grown-up.
Charmian	Oh, OK.

(Later)

Meera	(*Sings*) Dinner's coming, dinner's coming, are you ready? (*This is the song the children sing when they are waiting for the nursery lunch to be served.*)
Sharon	(*Nursery nurse, in the background*) Nursery, show me your hands! Hands! Come to me!
Meera	Show me your hands – everybody show me your hands!
Sharon	Right – now everyone come sit on the carpet for register.

Here Meera shows an ability to use English functionally, firstly to argue with Ebony about the organisation of the 'family' role play, and then to sound effectively teacher-like in the 'school' role play. More importantly it does not show Meera as a silent child who has nothing to contribute to classroom conversation. She contributes willingly, purposefully and appropriately.

In the second transcript, recorded in the writing area, we again noticed Meera's use of extended phrases to achieve an objective: in this case, to oversee the distribution of home language texts over which she seems to feel some kind of ownership.

Meera and Stefanie looking at Gujarati alphabet sheets – March 1995

Charmian   You can write on these if you want to.

Meera   Can I – can I write on *my* one?

Charmian   Mm hm.

Meera   I going to – I going to do it all by myself.

Charmian   Mm hm, well there's lots of them.

Stefanie   I want to do a (?) – a elephant.

Charmian   Mm hm. Can you find one?

(Stefanie looks through the photocopied alphabet sheets)

Meera   I can't – I can't – Stefanie can't have some more, I haven't got enough.

Charmian   There's lots and lots Meera, and I can make some more.

Meera   OK. Yes – I can get some to my sister?

Charmian   Yes, if you want.

Meera   You can keep this – this one for my sister.

Charmian   Do you want me to put it away safely then?

Meera   Yes, over there take it, and after my dinnertime.

Charmian   OK – fold it up – I'll put it here.

(Later, Meera suggests displaying the alphabet sheets on the wall in the role play area).

Meera   *(Pointing to the alphabet sheets)* Charmian, you can get some (?) and put it in the home corner if you want to. Stefanie – want to stick in the home corner – yes? Want this one? Charmian, can you put this one, put it up? *(To Stefanie)* You can get another one like this one, like me I got two of them.

Another extract from the same transcript demonstrates that Meera can use vivid description to tell a story. This was part of the 'chat' occurring whilst we worked together on the alphabet sheets, and may have been stimulated by the 'monster' subject of Stefanie's drawing.

(Stefanie asks me to look at her picture of a dinosaur.)

Meera   And Charmian –

Charmian   Yes?

Meera   What's that paper shop, and I bring some videos, and – and – bring it back, it's called a – there's a monster in there, it's – he's – making a (feet?) in my film.

Charmian   In your film?

Meera   Yeah, in the paper shop one, yeah!

Charmian   Yeah.

Meera   Yeah, and a monster break the car in there.

Charmian   Oh really!

Meera   And the children in there, he want to kill children and he's – blood in her face.

Charmian   Blood in her face – that sounds a bit too exciting!

In the above settings Meera was anything but a quiet, monosyllabic child. She reveals the ability to use a wide range of structures in her language, and more importantly is able to use them to sustain her part in an everyday conversation with all its variations. She does so with no apparent effort. She asks questions, signifies intentions, gives instructions, qualifies statements, makes assertions and offers narrations. As a consequence the dialogue is real conversation, not the truncated, one-sided talk that occurred in the book reading assessment situation.

Contexts for assessment

The above examples suggest that the context for talk affects the amount and variety of grammatical structures and vocabulary which Meera produces in English. Our discussion of the examples of transcript distinguished several possible factors which may be operating within the area of context: setting, time, relationships, and type of talk.

We agreed that socio-dramatic play settings enable bilingual children to explore, with their peers, a repertoire of language gleaned from everyday experience. However, the class teacher may not overhear the full sequence of such interactions.

Charmian	I was wondering whether what I've heard through being in this situation, sitting in a chair in the home corner... whether I've sort of eavesdropped in a way on different stuff from what you would hear going around the class as the teacher.
Helen	Well what I have read I'm enjoying because I think – I'm not sure – I think it's not what I hear, because I'm not there, I'm everywhere but not *there*...

The teacher's lack of time to spend in informal, extended conversation with children was highlighted in our discussion.

Charmian	I was wondering how often it's possible to assess children in this way – I mean presumably it's quite hard.
Kay	It's very time-consuming isn't it...? (*To Helen*) You and Sharon can talk to them about what they're doing, but haven't got time to sit and let them chat.
Helen	Yes, it's letting them chat –
Kay	That's what you just haven't got the time to access.
Helen	No, it's true, it's not just with them (*bilingual children*), it's with every single child, it's very limited.

Charmian's position as a researcher had given her the opportunity to participate in talk with the children on a relatively equal footing. Helen and Kay commented on the relationship with the children in the role play transcript:

Helen	Were you just observing this?
Charmian	I was just sitting in the home corner – it was all going on around me.
Helen	Just facilitating... It looks like you've managed to be there enough but not be in the way.
Kay	Of course they're sufficiently comfortable with you that they're relating to you as one of them – you're part of the peer group.

123

Meera's freedom to be directive with Charmian, both in role play and when working in the writing area, seemed to give rise to a considerable range of linguistic structures.

Helen   She's very confident with you, isn't she, she almost bosses you around.

Charmian   Oh yes, she does, definitely, not even almost! Which is interesting, because she then produces a lot of language which she would never say to a teacher.

We noted that for Meera, working with texts in Gujarati, which connected strongly with her home life, may have helped to change the power balance between herself and an adult in the nursery.

Charmian   She said to me the other day, 'I speak Gujarati, my Mum does, my Dad does, but Pinal doesn't, she speaks English'. (*Pinal is Meera's older sister*) – that's another thing she'll talk about of course, she'll talk about all the people in her family – that's another area of language, discussing literacy and spoken language.

Helen   And I think what you're bringing into the nursery, this kind of interest in *their* language... and how they use it, I think that is such a fantastic resource, I think that encourages them to talk.

During our discussion, we began to unravel the different ways in which an adult might approach talk with a child in the classroom, and how the approach might affect the child's response.

Charmian   It hadn't occurred to me before, but I wondered if, on the idea of assessment, they have some awareness that a teacher is in fact assessing them all the time in a way, and they don't think that I'm doing that.

Kay   I think I'm right in saying that most of the teacher-led discussion is questions and answers – What are you doing? Why are you doing it? What's going to happen next? You know – it's question question question answer. So in a way it is assessment.

124   **Helen**   ... just sort of naturally ...

Kay
: That's right, it's the way teachers talk, isn't it, you ask questions... It's something, you know, it's part of the breed almost, and in nursery in particular it must be quite new to them.

This led Helen to recall that one of the classroom helpers had turned down an invitation to participate in assessing talk, on the grounds that it would interfere with her relationship with the children. A nursery nurse had also decided to keep to her own more relaxed style of talk when working with children, pointing out that asking constant questions would interrupt the conversation and prevent exploration of anything other than 'teacher-type' language.

Aspects of language assessment

When we looked in more detail at Meera's spoken language, we focused on the areas of grammatical correctness and formality. Our individual professional backgrounds – as teacher of English as a second language, class teacher, and researcher – seemed to prompt us to consider different angles with regard to these topics.

Grammatical correctness

Kay saw a difference between the language structures used by Meera when being a 'teacher' in the role play, and the less 'correct' language produced when telling Charmian the story of the monster from the video.

Kay
: The only time her language is correct, and it's totally correct, is when she's in role as Helen or Sharon...but when you go on to what she's saying about the video, there's no comparison really, in the quality of what she's talking about....it's ideas, it's thoughts, she's conveying meaning....but it's almost like words for information, you put them together as best you can.

Helen
: As long as she's being understood, she's giving sufficient information even if it's not in the right way, she'll carry on using that – yes...

125

Kay's point is underlined by the moment when Meera directly imitates Sharon's instruction to 'show me your hands'. However, Charmian suggested another reason why Meera's story-telling language differed from her role-play language, and this was borne out by Helen's daily experience as the nursery teacher.

Charmian	I suppose it depends on how you see language though...because I was thinking with this (*the video story*), 'goodness, she can really say – get a lot across about what's going on in this video', and she was quite excited when she was saying it....
Helen	If you engage in something she's brought into school... she tends to get very excited, and will come out with that kind of language, almost like she is overflowing with excitement, and says 'Will you listen – erm, erm' – a bit like me now!... And if I sit down and ask questions to help her give me that information, break that down almost, she's then been able to use more appropriate sentences.

Here, Helen acknowledged the 'imperfect' nature of our own spoken language, as adults discussing a topic together. This raises the question of whether we tend to adopt more stringent criteria for assessing bilingual children's English than we would apply to the language of native speakers. Kay had already mentioned that Ebony's talk in the role plays was not always completely correct – for example, she says 'wiggle your hands up the air' – and Charmian remembered a tape of her son aged four, which had similarities to Meera's tale of the monster: 'he was telling a story, and quite a lot of it wasn't grammatically correct, but it was the flow of the story...' Charmian also noted that, where Meera's language might appear limited (for example, in organising the role play) it could be that the choice of words depended on the precise purpose Meera was intending to achieve.

Charmian	I mean look, she says 'you're the mum' and then 'you the auntie' and then 'you kid' – she knows perfectly well how to say it, but it may actually be a role, in a way, she's emphasising that she's ordering me around, whereas if you just happened to float past and hear her say 'you kid!' you could assume she doesn't know how to say 'you're the kid'.

Formality

We discussed how children are likely to adapt their language to the expectations of their listeners, with certain occasions requiring more formal constructions than others. Kay gave the example of 'sharing time', when children are asked to tell the whole group about items of news or information.

> **Kay** I think that's another time when children do tend to speak correctly – they're not babbling, they're not chatting, they're performing... even at nursery level, I get the impression they've got an awareness of specific language for specific occasions, and perhaps that links in with being the adult in role, the language for that occasion.
>
> **Helen** It's almost taking on the adult state, I mean the adult is usually sitting on the carpet with the children, talking and listening, and they're given the opportunity to do that...

Charmian saw potential difficulties in 'sharing time' talk: '... for some children it may be quite alarming, just because they have to stand up in front of people – it's not a common conversational everyday sort of situation really' – and suggested that children also need the chance to relax and explore language in less formal situations in the nursery. However, Helen pointed out that although sharing time is 'slightly false', it gives practice in turn-taking and awareness of other speakers, and Kay felt that more formal language *is* necessary for some everyday situations, such as discussing an illness with a doctor.

Ways forward

Our discussion has interesting connections with the work of other researchers. The tendency of teachers to operate largely through a stylised question and answer technique has been documented by Edwards and Westgate (1987), and Wells (1987) found that some children from non-mainstream backgrounds talked a great deal at home but were relatively silent when questioned by a teacher. The children studied by Tizard and Hughes (1984) who at home were non-stop talkers, went to nursery school and did not talk to their teachers: the teachers blamed this on the children's home background! A close examination of 'sharing time' in an urban United States classroom, by Michaels and Collins (1984), revealed that the children's language had to be formulated in a certain way in order to be acceptable to the teacher, and that contributions from children with a non-mainstream background, which were organised in a different style, tended not to be understood and followed up.

These research findings have general significance with regard to evaluation, but have particularly worrying implications for the performance of bilingual children. In contrast, Emblen (1990) has demonstrated how much a teacher researcher can discover about bilingual children's language competence through the natural conversation which arises when working on a classroom task with a group.

We discussed how contexts for assessment of talk in the nursery could be expanded to benefit children who have a different home language. Helen commented: 'The more I've been in this, the more I feel it's important not to make judgments until you've gathered all this kind of information in this way, that is watching and listening.'

She imagined how this could be done: 'If we had a whole load of little tapes and little video cameras even!' but noted the difficulties: 'It's been so often suggested as a means of getting an accurate record-keeping system in the nursery, but when I've sat down with a tape...it's quite hard to understand who's saying what.' Kay commented that, 'If you experience it, if you're part of it, you've got more idea.'

Whilst large-scale taping and transcription of bilingual children's talk would be an impossible addition to teachers' workloads, perhaps short stretches of time with a pocket audio-recorder in the role play area would be time well spent, with the chance to replay the tape as a reminder of the language heard. Paley, in her many books about young children (see, for example, Paley, 1984 and 1988), has shown just how illuminating the use of tape-recorded talk can be in an early years classroom. Involving other nursery workers in pooling their experience of talk with children could also be a way of building up a more well-rounded picture of bilingual children's abilities, just as we were doing in our conversation. It would be important to negotiate with each person to find an approach which they would feel comfortable about using, and which would not hamper the flexibility of interaction between themselves and the children. Taping the discussion between adults, as we did, could be a further aid to the evaluation procedure.

What was clear to all of us as a result of the discussion was that to evaluate any child's language use, one needs to listen to the child in a variety of contexts and in situations which offer the chance for children to utilise different language strengths. It is not sufficient simply to use situations which operate formally to assess language. In one sense to say this is to say nothing new; research has, as already indicated, highlighted this before. However, in days when teachers are under increasing pressure to make quick judgements, and when finding the time to listen to children in different contexts is increasingly difficult, it is important for us to insist as professionals that the point of evaluating children is to gain an accurate picture of their abilities. To do children justice and to help ourselves understand the children we teach, we need to offer them the means to reveal to us as many of their strengths as possible. Fairness to children demands that we are able to make adequate judgements about their language.

References

Biggs, A.P. and Edwards, V. (1994) 'I treat them all the same': Teacher–pupil talk in multiethnic classrooms, in Graddol, D.; Maybin, J. and Stierer B. (eds) *Researching Language and Literacy in Social Context.* Clevedon, Avon: Open University/Multilingual Matters.

Edwards, A.D. and Westgate, D.P.G. (1987) *Investigating Classroom Talk.* London: Falmer Press.

Emblen, V. (1990) 'Baby wasn't accident': The learning of pupils and teachers in natural conversation in an infant school in Levine J. (ed.) *Bilingual Learners and the Mainstream Curriculum.* Basingstoke, Hants.: Falmer Press.

Gregory, E. (1994) Negotiation as a criterial factor in learning to read in a second language in Graddol, D.; Maybin, J. and Stierer, B. (eds), op. cit.

Levine, J. (1990) Responding to linguistic and cultural diversity in the teaching of English as a second language in Levine, J. (ed), op. cit.

Michaels, S. and Collins, J. (1984) Oral discourse style: Classroom interaction and the acquisition of literacy in Tannen, D. (ed.) *Coherence in Written and Spoken Discourse.* Norwood, N.J.: Ablex.

Paley, V. (1984) *Boys and girls: superheroes in the doll corner.* Chicago: University of Chicago Press.

Paley, V. (1988) *Bad guys don't have birthdays: fantasy play at four.* Chicago: Chicago University Press.

Tizard B. and Hughes, M. (1984) *Young children learning: talking and thinking at home and school.* London: Fontana Books.

Wells, G. (1987) *The Meaning Makers.* London: Hodder and Stoughton.

Talk isn't always easy

10

Liz Jones

In this chapter I want to take one example of talk with a group of young children and explore why it was able to unsettle my stability as a teacher. This interaction with the children triggered a bundle of emotions including discomfort, unease and yet some excitement. It is these phenomena that I wish to understand. I want to understand them because, while we might all acknowledge both the value and power of talk between adults and children, for teachers 'talk isn't always easy'. Any potential obstacle is worth scrutinising.

My teaching career spans some twenty years and for the last six of them I have been working in a nursery. There is, then, a rich store of knowledge which I can plunder when confronted with pedagogical challenges. However, what I believe this example of talk reveals is that some of my teacher ways are informed by assumptions about, rather than insights into, the nature of children. Whilst I am an experienced teacher, my example firmly forbids feelings of complacency. The incident between myself and the children is like the stone that is thrown onto the flat, calm water of the pond. Ripples of disturbance have formed and it is these that I wish to understand.

I do a lot of talking in the nursery and it comes in many forms: I ask questions, try to communicate ideas, encourage, make demands, praise, chide, give information, describe, tell stories...

and much more. Talk and language development generally are the nuts and bolts of my craft. Given this, the question could be asked why, considering the amount of language development that is undertaken in the nursery, am I choosing to concentrate on one experience of talk with young children? The answer centres on two areas: one is the notion of control and my disquiet when I sense that my control is only tentative, and the other area is concerned with questioning the general belief that children's talk should be valued. The example highlights how this 'belief' is too wide a statement and that sometimes 'valuing' children's talk can be highly problematic. What I would like to do is deal first with notions of 'control', and then in a general way tease out some personal inhibitions which prevent me from fully valuing young children's talk.

There are many ways of defining what control is and implementing it. As a teacher, part of my professional remit is to be in control and to regulate the children. In my classroom there are very clear physical manifestations of overt control and regulation, for example, wall posters informing the class that 'only two children can play in the water' and picture clues on shelving and storage trays to ensure that the children replace equipment correctly. There are also covert forms of control which include conventions of behaviour towards each other. In the nursery, the children gradually acquire an appreciation of what constitutes a covert rule as a consequence of breaking the rule. For example, the children learn that shouting in the classroom is unacceptable because when they do it my face registers disapproval or I raise my fingers to my lips. The rule of no shouting is not implicitly stated; it is taught through mechanisms such as body language. Through the example of talk I want to examine whether the children have transgressed some of these covert rules which govern 'appropriate' language and behaviour.

Introducing the sample of talk

For the last four years I have been researching into my own teaching practice and my particular focus has been the language of the children. A recent research activity has been to monitor specific times during the day, including the first twenty minutes when school begins. By using procedures such as taped recordings of talk between myself and the children I try to capture moments of teaching practice which I can then reflect upon. The example of children's talk which is used in this chapter occurred at the beginning of the school day. It features three four-year-old girls: Hannah, Jessica and Amanda. The children are good friends and as a group they work well together. They often impress me with the ease and speed with which they construct stories and assign one another roles.

In an attempt to be approachable and less distant I have adopted the practice of sitting down each morning to welcome the children. Being the same height as the children has several advantages: I can hear what the children say, our eyes are on the same level so that we can 'read' each others faces, and I feel less formal. I shall be returning to this notion of 'less formal' later on in the chapter.

On this particular morning it was Hannah who arrived first and greeted me. Jessica and Amanda, however, followed close behind and were able to hear the initial exchange between Hannah and myself. To appreciate this story fully it is necessary to remember that my surname is Jones.

Hannah	Morning Mrs Dones.
LJ	Good morning Hannah.
Hannah	(*grinning broadly*) Good morning Mrs Dones Lones.
LJ	(*also grinning*) Good morning Lanna Danna.
Hannah	(*now concentrating*) Good morning Mrs Dones Lones Bones.
LJ	Good morning Lanna Danna Shanna.
Hannah	(*in a giggly, excited rush*) Good morning Mrs Jonesy Bonesy.
LJ	Good morning Mrs Hannah Panna.
Hannah	(*looking crestfallen*) I'm not a pan. You cook in a pan.
LJ	Well. I'm not just bones. I'm skin and bones.
Hannah	(*smiling once again*) Mrs Jones skin and bones. Mrs Jones skin and bones.
LJ	What else can we think of to rhyme with your name?... I know you can make Hannah and banana sound nearly the same.

Amanda	Do it with my name. Make my name say something.
LJ	(*also in a sing-song voice*) Amanda panda.
Hannah	There's a picture of a panda, Amanda (*and she points to the A-Z wall frieze where there is displayed a picture of a panda to illustrate and accompany the letter 'P'*).
Jessica	(*rhythmically*) Jessica messica pessica. Pessica messica Jessica.
LJ	That sounds like a train moving.

(I repeat Jessica's phrases and as I say the sounds I move my arms in a train motion. The three girls, Jessica, Hannah and Amanda, take off round the room, arms moving train-like chanting Jessica's phrase.)

Exploring the ripples of disturbances

What I will be documenting here are both my immediate reactions to this exchange and my later reflections. An initial reason for retaining this snapshot of teaching was because of vague feelings of nervousness during the actual interaction. This nervousness, I think, partly explains why I grin; my grinning covers my confusion. The process of understanding and exploring these vague feelings which I have referred to is a little like stripping an onion with each layer having the potential to reveal something about my teaching. This teasing apart is not a speedy process. It has taken several months involving many re-readings of the transcript thus allowing for 'different' interpretations. It is these interpretations or stories which are explored.

With her opening line of 'Morning Mrs Dones,' I think Hannah wanted some fun. My initial and troubled response was establishing what the nature of this 'fun' was and what my response should be. Was she inviting me to share her fun or was she making fun of me? Using a person's name as a mechanism for fun is a precarious business because it involves transgressing codes and practices which surround the activity of addressing people. These codes are not static, rigid rules; they change and alter to keep in step with societal changes. The manner by which adults and children address one another has its own history. The novel, *Jane Eyre* for example, gives us insights into the workings of the nineteenth-century bourgeois mind where school children and servants were kept firmly in their place through a variety of means including the practice of addressing them by surname only. During the 50s, when I was a child, it was standard practice to address unrelated but nevertheless familiar adults as 'aunt' or 'uncle' as a mark of respect. The way in which we address people is still a powerful mechanism for indicating respect, intimacy or social distance. These practices are guided by individual preferences and levels of tolerance and also what is customary for specific contexts.

As a teacher in the classroom my work is very public. The nursery door is always open and we have many visitors to the room. The first part of the morning is a particularly busy time of day when many of the children's parents and carers spend time with their children, sorting out the coats, putting names on the fruit, choosing a reading book to take home to share and generally settling their children. The exchange that took place between Hannah and myself was, in all likelihood, overheard by some of the parents. What will be their view? Will they read Hannah's greeting as an indication that I lack rigour and have as a consequence insufficient control over the children? Do they hold fixed or flexible views on how young children should speak to adults in general and particularly to teachers? Will they think that Hannah's act is that of an imaginative child or a rude one? Whilst I might never know the answers to these questions, Hannah's opening remark prompts me to examine whether I have the right balance. I want to be an approachable, informal teacher, yet I must still command respect from the children that I teach and from their parents.

Hannah, by referring to me as Mrs Dones, does two things: first, she tampers with my name and second, she strays from the usual procedure by which the young children of my class address me. I have already indicated how forms of address can be problematic. In deviating from the routine form of address Hannah forces me to recognise that I juggle between two positions. On the one hand I perceive myself as an approachable teacher who has considered how she can make herself more available to the children (a 'listening teacher') but one who is clearly phased when a child opts to follow her own agenda. It is possible, by carefully examining this small example, to track my ambivalence and general discomfort.

Hannah opens the exchange between us with 'Morning Mrs Dones'. My reply of 'Good morning Hannah' tries to achieve several things. First, I ignore Hannah's deliberate corruption of my name, working on the ploy that if something is ignored it might disappear. But what I also try to do is to remind Hannah that there are conventions which surround teacher–child exchanges and to indicate that she has deviated from them.

As is evident from the example, Hannah is not deterred; instead, she extends and elaborates the name play. At this juncture it would have been possible for me to invoke my teacher authority and close all further exchanges between us. However, as the transcript shows I chose not to do this, preferring to continue the 'game'. One reason for wanting to participate stems from a set of teacher beliefs which values the child's own ideas and language. But I also recognise that my decision to become part of the game was so that I could exercise control over its development; for example, I use the question, 'What else can we think of to rhyme with your name?' as a brake on the child's flow. This question serves two functions: it gives the exchange between Hannah and myself a veneer of educational worthiness, and it directs the child's attention away from my name.

So far I have ignored Amanda's and Jessica's part in the exchange; it is here that I want to concentrate on their contributions. Amanda and Jessica are, for a while, observers. It would appear that the girls have not been passive onlookers but that they have been following and taking note of the exchange between their friend and their teacher. It is possible that Amanda, in wanting me to do 'it' with her name, has fathomed the thinking that underpins the word play. Her request to me could be a signal that she wants to participate in the play and she offers her own name as an entry ticket into the game. This could suggest that Amanda has no difficulties or worries in offering her name as a springboard. Perhaps this is because Amanda, unlike me, has through careful observation taken note of Hannah's crestfallen face when I referred to her as 'Hannah panna' and that she has 'read' Hannah's words of 'I'm not a pan. You cook in a pan' as an oblique and covert rule inserted to curb the possible power of the game to wound.

When Jessica enters into the exchange she does so by taking her name and playing with the initial letter: 'Jessica, messica, pessica'. In addition, she adds the dimension of rhythm. I pick up on this and suggest the idea of a train. It is possible to bring different readings to this contribution of 'a train'. One reading could be that I'm building on from Jessica's contribution and that I am helping the children to extend and develop their ideas. What the children and I have established is a partnership which allows us to collaborate and pool ideas. However, there is an alternative reading: it could be that through introducing the idea of a train my intention was not to collaborate, rather it was to direct and as a consequence assume more control. The train effectively took the girls' attention away from rhyming words and put an end to the game. Furthermore, the train added a physical dimension and as a consequence removed the focus from a verbal one.

Calmer waters?

This heading might suggest that because I have subjected an aspect of my teaching to a fairly rigorous scrutiny, 'talk' will now be easy! The question mark is there to throw doubt on such a hope.

I know that I want the children in my class to talk to me. I know that I will continue to think of inventive ways of 'managing' myself and the classroom generally so that I can create more opportunities for the children to have conversations with me. What I am less certain about is whether it is possible to completely eradicate those assumptions and ingrained views and prejudices that, for a variety of personal and cultural reasons, impinge on and affect my teaching and, more specifically, the way I talk to the children. However, whilst I am pessimistic about the possibilities of completely freeing myself from the shackles of conventions, traditions and the like, I know that I should never stop trying.

Do I really want calm waters? If calm waters means feeling excitement, elation and for some of the time, satisfaction with aspects of my teaching then I certainly want to be upon calmer waters. However, if it implies a flatness with no ripples of change to disturb the surface, then I must reject them. In this instance, by focusing on one example of talk I have moved from mere description to understanding the complexities of such descriptions, a process that could not happen without making waves. By trying to describe an example of talk and then reflecting on the description, I now at least have the opportunity to ask the question, 'Now where?'